ESSENTIAL ELEMENTS
FOR STRINGS
A COMPREHENSIVE STRING METHOD

MICHAEL ALLEN • ROBERT GILLESPIE • PAMELA TELLEJOHN HAYES
ARRANGEMENTS BY JOHN HIGGINS

ESSENTIAL ELEMENTS INCLUDES:

Comprehensive Pedagogy
• Address the *process* of teaching and learning.

Review Section
• Ideal refresher of Book 1 essentials.

Flexible Sequence Format
• Teach any skill at any time, organized with easy-to-read tab sections.

Key Centered Pedagogy
• New notes taught within the context of a complete scale.

Finger Patterns
• Comprehensive studies grouped by pattern, by string, and by key.

Integrated Curriculum
• Theory, history, and multiculturalism in the examples.

Innovative Rhythm System
• Graphics, subdivision, and easy-to-learn sequence.

Broad Musical Spectrum
• Classics to contemporary-designed to motivate.

AVAILABLE PUBLICATIONS

Violin	Piano Accompaniment
Viola	Play-Along CDs
Cello	EE String Orchestra Series
Double Bass	

ISBN 978-0-634-05263-7
Copyright © 2004 by HAL LEONARD CORPORATION
International Copyright Secured   All Rights Reserved

HAL•LEONARD®
CORPORATION
7777 W. BLUEMOUND RD. P.O. BOX 13819 MILWAUKEE, WI 53213

TABLE OF CONTENTS

The *Essential Elements for Strings* Teacher's Manual Book 2 is designed to serve as a resource for all your string teaching needs. It contains teaching tips, sample letters for communicating with parents, sample test forms for evaluating students' playing skills, and words to some of the familiar melodies in the book.

SEQUENCE OF

	1	2	3	4	5	6	7	8	9	10	11	12
Teacher Page												
Student Page	1	2	3	4	5	6	7	8	9	10	11	12
Bowings		Slur, Legato Bowing	Bow Lift '	♩	⌐⌐	♩	Tone Production	Changing Bow Speed	Shadow Bowing		♩. ♪	
Rhythms		o, ♩, ♪	♩. ♫					♩. ♪	♪ ⁊ ⁊ ♪	♩. ♪		
Theory		D Major Key Signature, 4/4, Major Scale	3/4, Repeat Sign, Tie, 1st & 2nd Endings	G Major, Interval	G Major, Upper Octave	C Major, 2/4	C Time Signature			Counting ♩. ♪ 1 & 2 & ⌢		
History			Edvard Grieg									
Terms		Legato, Major Scale	Dynamics: *p*, *f* cresc., decresc. Moderato, Incidental Music	Andante	Allegro, Intonation	Allegretto	Dynamics: *mp*, *mf*			Fermata	Lento Andantino	
Listening Skills												C#
Familiar Melodies		Theme from London Symphony	Morning from Peer Gynt, Barcarolle	Chester		Buffalo Gals		Alouette, Rigaudon, Oh! Susannah	Jesse James		A Capital Ship, Theme from New World Symphony, Rondeau	At Pierrot's Door, Hot Cross Buns
Special Features	Welcome Table of Contents	Tuning Track	Left Hand Shape and Pre-Shifting Workouts			C Major Lower Octave (Viola, Cello),		Essential Creativity: Choosing Dynamics	♪ ⁊ ⁊ ♪ Rhythm Rap	♩. ♪ Rhythm Rap	Essential Creativity: Choosing Rhythms	3-4 Finger Pattern (Violin, Viola), Forward Extension (Cello)
Quiz Assessments				✓ Left Hand Shape		✓ Bow Hand Shape			*mf*, Crescendo Decrescendo ♪⁊		♩. ♪, Hooked Bowing, Ritardando	✓ Checking C# Intonation
Note Sequence — Violin											♯♩	
Viola											♯♩	
Cello											♯♩	
Bass												

ESSENTIAL ELEMENTS

	13	14	15	16	17	18	19	20	21	22	23	24
Teacher Page												
Student Page	13	14	15	16	17	18	19	20	21	22	23	24
Bowings			[bowing marks]			[bowing notation]						
Rhythms				[16th notes]	[16th notes]		[syncopation notation]					
Theory	A Major Key Signature			Counting [16th notes] 1 e & a	Counting [16th notes] 1 & a / 1 e &	Counting [notation] 1e&a	Counting [notation] 1 & 2 &		F Major Key Signature		Bb Major Key Signature	
History		Nationalistic Music										
Terms							Syncopation		Concerto			
Listening Skills	G#	F#	G#					Bb	F♮			Bb, Eb
Familiar Melodies		Russian Folk Tune	Sitka City	Dinah Won't You Blow Your Horn, Mockingbird			Children's Shoes, Tom Dooley	Rolling Along	Theme From Violin Concerto	Hot Cross Buns		
Special Features	3-4 Finger Pattern on D String (Violin, Viola) Forward Extension (Cello) 1/2 position on G String (Bass)	F# on C String (Viola) Forward Extention (Cello)	G# on E String (Violin, Bass) Upper Octave A Major Scale (Violin)	Rhythm Rap	Rhythm Rap, Rhythm Rap	Rhythm Rap, Essential Creativity: Writing D Major Scale Using 16th Note Rhythms	Rhythm Rap	Low First Finger Pattern (Violin) Bb on G String (Viola, Cello) 1/2 position on A String (Bass)	Low First Finger Pattern On E String (Violin) 1/2 position on E Sring (Bass)	Low First Finger on D String (Violin, Viola), Low First Finger on A String (Viola), Bb on G String (Violin), Backward Extension (Cello), 1/2 position on D & G Strings (Bass)	Slovakian Folk Song, Ayn Kaylokaynu	Low Fourth Finger Pattern on E String (Violin), Low Fourth Finger Pattern on A String (Violin, Viola), Special Writing Exercise (Cello, Bass)
Quiz Assessments	Key of A Major, C# on G String, G# on D String, Forward Extension (Cello), 4th Finger on G String (Violin, Viola)				[16th note groupings] Counting 16th Notes		[notation]				Hooked Bowing, Key of Bb Major, A Tempo, Fermata, Fourth Finger on G String (Violin, Viola)	
Note Sequence — Violin	[staff notation]		[staff notation]					[staff notation]	[staff notation]	[staff notation]		[staff notation]
Viola	[staff notation]		[staff notation]					[staff notation]		[staff notation]		[staff notation]
Cello	[staff notation]		[staff notation]					[staff notation]		[staff notation]		
Bass	[staff notation]		[staff notation]					[staff notation]	[staff notation]	[staff notation]		

SEQUENCE OF

Teacher Page												
Student Page	**25**	**26**	**27**	**28**	**29**	**30**	**31**	**32**	**33**	**34**	**35**	**36**
Bowings												
Rhythms						Mixed Meter	♪♪♪ (3)					
Theory	B♭ Major Scale Upper Octave	6/8, Round	Counting in Two 6/8	Minor Scales, D Minor (Natural) Scale	G Minor Key Signature, G Minor (Natural) Scale		Counting ♪♪♪ (3) 1-trip-let	Counting ¢ Time				
History			Mozart	Mahler					Cantatas			Holst
Terms		Round				Cantabile, Italian "e"						
Listening Skills												
Familiar Melodies	The Mountain Deer Chase, Rakes Of Mallow	Row, Row, Row Your Boat, Jolly Good Fellow	May Time	Mahler's Theme, Shalom Chaverim, The Snake Charmer	Hatikvah, The Hanukkah Song	French Folk Song, Kum Ba Yah	Field Song	When The Saints Go Marchin' In	March From Peasant's Cantata	Streets Of Laredo, Yellow Rose Of Texas	Pomp And Circumstance, America The Beautiful	La Bamba, In The Bleak Midwinter
Special Features	Essential Creativity: Changing Rhythms and Phrases			Minor Scales	Israeli National Anthem, Upper and Lower Octave G Minor (Natural) Scale (Violin)		♪♪♪ (3) Rhythm Rap	¢♩♪♪♪♪, ♩♩ Rhythm Rap, ¢♩. ♩, ♩♩. Rhythm Rap	¢♩ ♪ Rhythm Rap, ¢♩ ♪♪♪♪ Rhythm Rap	Performance Spotlight, Orchestra Arrangement	Performance Spotlight, Orchestra Arrangement	Performance Spotlight, Orchestra Arrangement
Quiz Assessments					Key of G minor, B♭, E♭, Dynamics			✓ Counting in Cut Time				
Note Sequence Violin												
Viola												
Cello												
Bass												

ESSENTIAL ELEMENTS

	37	38	39	40	41	42	43	44	45	46	47	48
Teacher Page												
Student Page	37	38	39	40	41	42	43	44	45	46	47	48
Bowings												
Rhythms												
Theory			Natural Harmonic							Improvisation, Composition		
History												
Terms		Sight-Reading	Shifting							Improvisation, Composition	Double Stops	
Listening Skills												
Familiar Melodies	Swallowtail Jig											
Special Features	Performance Spotlight, Orchestra Arrangement	Principles of Sight-reading	Preparing for Higher Positions, Playing Natural Harmonics, Shifting	Finger Patterns: Organized by Pattern (Violin, Viola)	Finger Patterns: Organized by String (Violin, Viola)	Finger Patterns: Organized by Key: C, G, D Major (Violin, Viola)	Finger Patterns: Organized by Key: A, F, B♭ Major (Violin, Viola)	Scales and Arpeggios: C, G, D, A Major	Scales and Arpeggios: F, B♭ Major D, G Minor (Natural)	Improvising and Composing Musical Phrases, Question and Answer Phrases	Simple Double Stops, Fingering Chart	EE Reference Index
Quiz Assessments								✓ Identifying Elements of Performing Scales and Arpeggios				
Note Sequence												
Violin												
Viola												
Cello												
Bass												

USING ESSENTIAL ELEMENTS FOR STRINGS

Essential Elements for Strings is a comprehensive method for string musicians, and can be used with heterogeneous and homogeneous classes or individuals. It is designed with fail-safe options for teachers to customize the learning program to meet their changing needs.

The Teacher's Manual includes all the music and text from the student books, plus timesaving teaching tips throughout the score. As in the student books, a color box always highlights the introduction of a new concept.

TABS

Tabs appear on the side of each page to help find topics quickly and easily. In that way you may use the pages consecutively or in an order you choose.

KEYS

D Major – two octaves for viola and cello
G Major – two octaves for violin
C Major – two octaves for viola and cello
A Major – two octaves for violin
F Major – one octave
Bb Major – two octaves for violin
D Minor (Natural) – two octaves for viola and cello
G Minor (Natural) – two octaves for violin

RHYTHMS

3/4 Meter
Eighth notes/eighth rests
Dotted notes
Sixteenth notes
Syncopation
6/8 Meter
Mixed meter
Cut time
Triplets

LISTENING SKILLS

Listening Skills are included every time a new note is introduced. Research suggests that students with well-developed listening skills have better left/right hand coordination, intonation, and memorization skills. Sample four-beat patterns are provided so teachers may play patterns for students to echo.

RHYTHM RAPS

After establishing the quarter note pulse, all new rhythms are presented in the innovative *Rhythm Rap* format. Each *Rhythm Rap* may be clapped, tapped, counted aloud or silently, shadow bowed (bowed in the air), or bowed on an open string, or played with the accompanying tracks. After each *Rhythm Rap*, the identical rhythms are played on simple pitches in the next exercise.

Also note that all Rhythm Raps and correlated melodies are first presented in D Major, the key most familiar to students. This is designed so students only have to learn one new concept at a time.

PLAY-ALONG TRACKS

Play-along tracks are available for every exercise in the book.

For classroom use, the *Teacher's Manual* includes a play-along CD for exercises 1–71, with a small string ensemble demonstrating the melody part. All tracks are available for teachers and students at www.myeelibrary.com.

Each track is played twice—the second time is the accompaniment only. There is a one measure count-off before each track, with metronome clicks that are subdivided by soft cymbal notes. These tracks are performed on real instruments that support phrasing and dynamics, teaching musicality from the start. They explore a rich variety of musical styles and cultures, including classical, rock, jazz, country, and world music.

PERFORMANCE SPOTLIGHT

A special section of arrangements appears on student book pages 34–37. These pieces may be used in a special concert performance, or at any time you choose once students have mastered the necessary playing skills. Different styles of music are included to provide a varied musical experience for both the audience and performers.

FINGER PATTERNS

A special section for developing violin and viola students' finger patterns, organized by pattern, string, and key.

SCALES

Special pages for reviewing and practicing all scales and arpeggios are presented.

SHIFTING

Rote *Workout* exercises encourage left hand mobility. Shifting is introduced using harmonics.

SIGHT-READING

A special **STAR** acronym is used for introducing strategies for teaching students basic sight-reading strategies. This is followed by *Sight-Reading Challenges* in a variety of keys and rhythms.

MUSIC THEORY, HISTORY, AND CROSS-CURRICULAR ACTIVITIES

All the necessary materials are woven into the learning program in the student books. With teaching time in short supply, this makes it more practical to relate music to history, world cultures or to other subjects in the curriculum. These *Theory* and *History* features are highlighted by **color** boxes and appear throughout the book.

As a result, teachers can efficiently meet and exceed the **National Standards for Arts Education**, while still having the time to focus on music performance skills.

CREATIVITY

Essential Creativity exercises appear throughout the book. They are designed to stimulate imaginations and to foster a creative attitude toward music. Included among exercises are activities for composing and improvising music. Additional suggestions are included in the *Teacher's Manual*.

ASSESSMENT

ESSENTIAL ELEMENTS QUIZZES

Student playing quizzes appear throughout the books. Objectives highlight the exact elements being reviewed and tested. Review exercises in the Teacher's Manual suggest specific examples for students requiring additional practice. Be certain students meet your performance expectations on every quiz.

A **Star Achiever** chart is provided in the Teacher's Manual. It lists all the Essential Elements Quizzes and Essential Creativity exercises. This chart should be reproduced and distributed to each student.

EE CHECKS ✓

EE Checks appear throughout the book. They are special reminders for students to evaluate the playing skills that have just been introduced.

Additional Resources Available...

PIANO ACCOMPANIMENT BOOK

Piano accompaniments for each exercise are provided in a separate book, but are also printed in the *Teacher's Manual*. These easy accompaniments have been arranged to match the style and harmony of the accompaniments heard on the play-along tracks. They may be used for teaching or performance and offer a variety of styles, from classical to contemporary popular music. You may want to alter these piano accompaniments to meet your specific needs.

ORCHESTRA DIRECTOR COMMUNICATION KIT

This book offers 32 reproducible letters on CD ROM format for easy use. It includes letters on music advocacy, the benefits of musical study in the development of the child, and a variety of subjects that apply to the orchestra classroom.

ESSENTIAL ELEMENTS FOR STRINGS BOOK 2
TECHNIQUE SEQUENCE

The following chart outlines the technique sequence for developing students' playing skills.

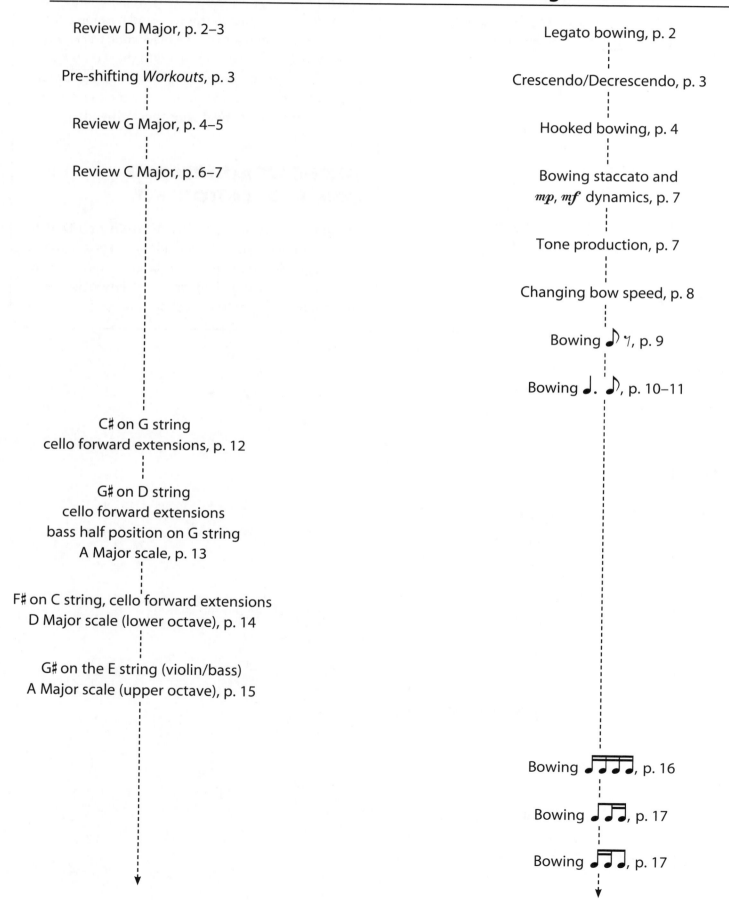

Left Hand Skills

Review D Major, p. 2–3

Pre-shifting *Workouts*, p. 3

Review G Major, p. 4–5

Review C Major, p. 6–7

C♯ on G string
cello forward extensions, p. 12

G♯ on D string
cello forward extensions
bass half position on G string
A Major scale, p. 13

F♯ on C string, cello forward extensions
D Major scale (lower octave), p. 14

G♯ on the E string (violin/bass)
A Major scale (upper octave), p. 15

Right Hand Skills

Legato bowing, p. 2

Crescendo/Decrescendo, p. 3

Hooked bowing, p. 4

Bowing staccato and
mp, *mf* dynamics, p. 7

Tone production, p. 7

Changing bow speed, p. 8

Bowing ♪ ⅞, p. 9

Bowing ♩. ♪, p. 10–11

Bowing ♫♫, p. 16

Bowing ♩♫, p. 17

Bowing ♫♩, p. 17

Left Hand Skills

Right Hand Skills

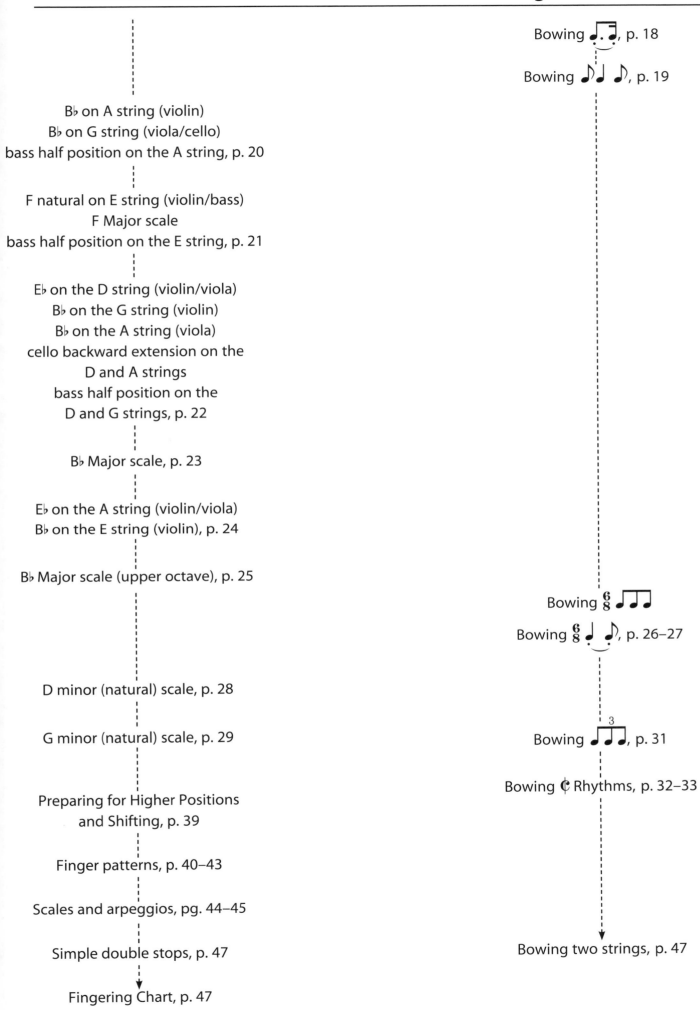

Bowing ♩. ♩, p. 18

Bowing ♪♩ ♪, p. 19

B♭ on A string (violin)
B♭ on G string (viola/cello)
bass half position on the A string, p. 20

F natural on E string (violin/bass)
F Major scale
bass half position on the E string, p. 21

E♭ on the D string (violin/viola)
B♭ on the G string (violin)
B♭ on the A string (viola)
cello backward extension on the
D and A strings
bass half position on the
D and G strings, p. 22

B♭ Major scale, p. 23

E♭ on the A string (violin/viola)
B♭ on the E string (violin), p. 24

B♭ Major scale (upper octave), p. 25

Bowing 6/8 ♩♩♩

Bowing 6/8 ♩ ♪, p. 26–27

D minor (natural) scale, p. 28

G minor (natural) scale, p. 29

Bowing ♩♩♩ (3), p. 31

Bowing ¢ Rhythms, p. 32–33

Preparing for Higher Positions
and Shifting, p. 39

Finger patterns, p. 40–43

Scales and arpeggios, pg. 44–45

Simple double stops, p. 47

Bowing two strings, p. 47

Fingering Chart, p. 47

PARENT COMMUNICATION & STUDENT EVALUATION

Communication with parents is an essential element of a successful orchestra program. The following letters provide valuable information for orchestra parents. Feel free to make copies of the letters for use in your program. Or, you may want to adapt the letters to meet the individual needs of your program in a different way.* Letters on different topics for communicating with parents are included in *Essential Elements for Strings Teacher's Manual Book 1* and the *Essential Elements Orchestra Director's Communication Kit*.

*Editable text files for the letters and evaluations in this book are available in the Teacher Resource Kit, Book 2 (CD-ROM), HL #00868133.

Topics of Letters for *Teacher's Manual Book 2*:

- Encouragement following the first three to six weeks of instruction

- Encouragement following the first three to four months of instruction

- Guidelines for purchasing an instrument

- Instrument maintenance

- When a student is considering dropping out

- Enrolling in next year's string/orchestra class

- Encouragement for private lessons

- Importance of involving students in other outside-of-school music activities

- When a student wants to change instruments

- Practice suggestions and ways parents can monitor student practice at home

Sample Test Forms: *Teacher's Manual Book 2*:

Evaluating students is an important part of the teaching process and validates the content of string class instruction to parents and school administrators. The following sample test forms are included for your use and adaptation. Feel free to make photocopies for your use.

The test forms in the *Teacher's Manual* are the following:

- General Performance Evaluation

- Détaché Bowing Skills Quiz

- Instrument & Left Hand Position Quiz

- Scale Test

- Playing Quiz: #36 Jesse James

- Playing Quiz: #47 Rondeau

- A Major Scale Quiz

DATELINE: Send 3–6 weeks into *Essential Elements for Strings Book 2*

Dear Parents:

It is time to share a positive report with you about the ongoing success of our orchestra program and the important contribution your child is making to the group. You must be very proud of (his/her) continued mastery of the instrument.

The language of music has no boundaries. In the formative years of orchestra, we often overlook this extraordinary communication tool. It is easy to get caught up in the technical calisthenics of learning to play the instrument and lose sight of the real purpose in choosing the study of music.

A high level of proficiency creates a higher expectancy from each member of the organization. The goals of orchestra are now more advanced, and thus the attainment of these objectives requires a greater sense of commitment from every member. Your encouragement is a key factor in this endeavor. Persistence is absolutely necessary for forward progress. Establishing daily practice habits will ensure personal success for your child.

As always, you are encouraged to share your thoughts concerning the progress of your child and the growth of the (name of school) orchestra. Thank you for your support in this meaningful learning experience for all of the students. I look forward to having you with us at our next concert (date/time/place).

Sincerely,

Orchestra Teacher

DATELINE: Send 3–4 months into *Essential Elements for Strings Book 2*

Dear Parents:

The benefits of orchestra extend far beyond the mastery and understanding of musical technique. The nurturing of a positive self-image is a certain reward for any student who plays an active role in the orchestra. Ongoing research confirms that music students score higher in academic subjects and are actively sought by colleges and universities, not only for their musical talents, but also because they rank at the top of their classes in school.

Ultimately, music study helps young people to be successful in life through the musical and non-musical benefits they receive. The study of music enhances their future. It affords them the opportunity to reach their potential and enjoy the achievement of both personal and group goals.

The College Entrance Examination Board announced that in 1996, students who studied arts and music scored significantly higher than the national average on the Scholastic Aptitude Test. Students who participated in acting/play production, music performance and appreciation, drama appreciation, and arts history scored an average of 31 to 50 points higher for the math and verbal sections of the test. The Board also stated that students with long-term arts study (four years or more) tend to score significantly higher on the SAT than those with less course work in the arts.

I cannot overstate the advantages of your child's continued involvement in orchestra. It is an investment that will continue to pay tremendous dividends for your child's future.

Sincerely,

Orchestra Teacher

DATELINE: Purchasing an instrument

Dear Parents:

Students need a quality string instrument that sounds good. Research shows that the unique sounds of string instruments are one of the most frequently cited reasons for enrolling in string classes. However, when students are considering dropping strings, one of the most frequently cited reasons is having an instrument that is in poor repair and difficult to play.

Purchasing a string instrument is just like purchasing an automobile. You most often pay for what you get, and you need to buy from reputable dealers and companies. The quality of string instruments varies from A to Z, as does the purchase price. Typically the more you pay for an instrument the better it will sound and the easier it is to play.

When purchasing an instrument there are some guidelines to follow. Be sure the instrument meets the string instrument guidelines established by the Music Educators National Conference. These instrument specifications are designed to ensure that the instrument meets minimum industry standards. Next, the instrument must be the correct size for your child. String instruments come in many different lengths and must fit your child. If your child plays the wrong sized instrument, (he/she) will develop many poor posture and playing habits that will limit (his/her) progress. I can size your child accurately. Please contact me before selecting an instrument.

Purchase an instrument only from a recognized string instrument company or dealer that sells and repairs violins, violas, cellos, and basses on a regular basis. There are unique characteristics to bowed string instruments that the company that you are dealing with must be competent in handling.

Above all, as with any major purchase, please contact me well in advance of purchasing an instrument so that I may assist you. I know best the playing skills and instrument needs of your child. String instruments prices vary greatly, from $100 to more than $1,000,000, and most often keep their value. I will be happy to advise you in getting the most appropriate instrument for your child. Thank you for your support, and I look forward to working with you in this most important purchase.

Sincerely,

Orchestra Teacher

DATELINE: Instrument maintenance. Send as needed

To the parents of:

_____

     A well maintained instrument and equipment is essential for your child's progress. An instrument in need of repair prevents your child from doing well in class. The checklist below is for your assistance. Contact me if you need suggestions on where repairs can be made. When the necessary items have been corrected, please return this sheet to me.

_____ String(s) need to be replaced. Strings wear out and need to be replaced even if they are not broken.

_____ Clean and polish instrument body. USE ONLY POLISH MADE ESPECIALLY FOR STRINGED INSTRUMENTS THAT IS AVAILABLE AT A STRING INSTRUMENT SHOP.

_____ A soft cloth is needed to keep in the case. Students should wipe off the instrument and bow each time after they are done playing. This will prevent dirt and rosin buildup that can damage the instrument.

_____ Bridge needs to be replaced. Please be sure a repairman properly fits the bridge. You must take the instrument with you to the string shop. Simply buying a bridge will not solve the problem.

_____ Soundpost must be set-up and adjusted inside the instrument. Only a knowledgeable string repairman can do this.

_____ A shoulder pad is needed to support the violin/viola properly. The student should take (his/her) instrument to the string instrument store to be fitted.

_____ A rock stop is needed or needs to be replaced.

_____ The bow needs to be rehaired. Bow hair wears out. It needs to be replaced at least once a year.

_____ The fine tuner needs to be repaired or replaced. Violins, violas, and cellos should have fine tuners that work easily for each string.

_____ Repair or replace bass stool. Bass stools do wear out, and the height of the stool needs to change as the student grows taller.

_____ Other:

    Remember to have your child return this letter to me when the above item(s) have been corrected or replaced. Please feel free to contact me for additional information if necessary.

                                      Sincerely,

                                      Orchestra Teacher

Date notified: _____

Date corrected: _____

Parent's Signature _____

DATELINE: When a student is considering dropping out

Dear (Name of Parent):

Your child has expressed a desire to drop out of the orchestra program. Perhaps (he/she) has discussed this with you. This is a serious decision that will not only affect (his/her) musical progress, but also other areas of growth as well.

Participation in an orchestra program gives students a hands-on approach to the arts, allowing them to experience music by some of the world's greatest composers. In addition, consistent practice on a string instrument fosters self-discipline that will affect all other areas of study for the rest of (his/her) life. Disciplined work habits developed in practice will also help their other academic studies. Orchestra students consistently place in the top ten percent of their high school class. Playing a string instrument well also gives students special opportunities for achievement and recognition through performing, both for their parents and peers.

Please try to determine specifically why your child has lost interest in playing. Pinpointing the reason will help us find an answer. There are many possible solutions through increased attention, recognition, rewards, instruction, and encouragement. Let's find the best combination to help your child.

Please contact me at your earliest convenience so that we can best keep a special place for your child in the orchestra and protect (his/her) future.

Sincerely,

Orchestra Teacher

DATELINE: Enrolling in next year's orchestra class

Dear Parents:

Soon it will be time for your child to schedule (his/her) classes for next year. (Name of child) has been a special part of our orchestra, and the other students and I look forward to (him/her) being with us next year.

Orchestra is a unique class where students learn to work together for a common goal and learn the importance of teamwork. They learn to respect their peers and develop friendships as they develop their playing skills and perform successfully in concerts. The self-discipline developed in consistent string instrument practice affects all areas of a child's future and helps them work to set and achieve goals for themselves, two important life skills. Music students typically score higher on college entrance exams such as the SAT, and many colleges offer scholarships to string players, for both the music major and the non-music major. The recognition that a child feels in successfully playing a string instrument helps (him/her) grow in self-confidence and results in a healthy self-esteem and feeling of personal worth, which are critical for life's future challenges.

String study in orchestra opens many doors for a child and helps prepare them for the future. Please be certain that those in charge of scheduling your child's classes for next year know that your child will be enrolling in orchestra. If I can be of any assistance in this or anything else regarding your child, please do not hesitate to contact me at your earliest convenience. We are a team working on behalf of your child.

Sincerely,

Orchestra Teacher

DATELINE: Encouraging private instruction as supplement to orchestra instruction

Dear Parents:

Opportunities for private instruction for our orchestra members are now available. The individual attention that a student receives in private instruction helps develop (his/her) unique maximum potential as a player and member of our orchestra. In addition, private instruction offers students the opportunity to explore the extensive wealth of solo literature available for their instrument. All of the world's greatest composers have written masterpieces for each of the string instruments, and private lessons give students the opportunity to explore and experience them. Private lessons also provide special performing opportunities that bring recognition for your child through solo recitals.

The private string teachers available to teach students in our orchestra program are recommended because of their teaching success with young people. They are working toward the same goals of the orchestra program and understand how to motivate and teach your child to be able to reach (his/her) special talent on a string instrument. Please contact the private teacher of your choice for further details.

Giving students private lessons is one very effective way to enrich a child's string experience. Many of the most outstanding players in our orchestra program study privately and have become our leaders. Please seriously consider offering this special opportunity to your child. Please contact me so that we may discuss this further.

Sincerely,

Orchestra Teacher

DATELINE: Encouraging student involvement in outside-of-school music activities

Dear Parents:

Your child is making excellent progress on (his/her) string instrument and is playing extremely well. Bravo to both you and your child! Since your child is doing so well, I wanted to inform you of other enriching outside-of-school music activities that are available to string students to supplement their school orchestra experience.

Summer orchestra camps are available which offer unique experiences for children who play string instruments. These camps are designed to build upon the skills students have learned in class during the school year and provide opportunities to meet fellow string students from throughout the state, coupled with many recreational and sports activities. These newly developed skills and friends go a long way in motivating and sustaining the interests of students in string study during the summer months in a fun, non-competitive setting. Contact me about enrollment details.

Attending concerts during the year with your child, in addition to our school programs, enriches (his/her) musical appreciation and shows (him/her) your essential support of (his/her) music study. Our area offers many fine concerts that are interesting and educational to attend. I will inform the students of special performances and watch the newspapers for concert information.

Listen to recordings of string and orchestra music at home and purchase additional music for your child to play. These are activities that will help your child explore other music and deepen their love of music. Such activities are enjoyable, and the entire family can benefit. Contact me for a list of suggested recordings and music, or ask your child's private lesson teacher, if they are studying privately.

Playing a string instrument in a school orchestra opens up many opportunities for musical experiences that enrich a child's life. Please let me know if I can help you and your child find additional musical resources.

Sincerely,

Orchestra Teacher

DATELINE: When students want to change instruments

Dear Parents:

Your child has expressed interest in learning to play a different string instrument. This is a serious issue and warrants careful consideration. There are important matters to consider.

Your child has spent time and worked hard developing playing skills on (his/her) current instrument. Some of these skills will transfer to another instrument, but not all. Students have to realize that in many ways they will be a beginner on the new instrument, and it will be like starting over. They need to consider the effort it will take to develop fundamental skills to play the new instrument well, and the practicing it will require to keep up with their friends in orchestra on their new instrument.

Changing instruments in the string family frequently means learning a new music clef, which will require effort to develop note-reading skills for the new instrument. Violin music is written in treble clef, viola music in alto clef, and cello and bass music in bass clef. Students need to realize that in addition to learning the unique technical skills on a different string instrument, they probably will have to learn a new note reading system as well.

Many issues are involved and important to discuss when students want to change to a different instrument. Please contact me as soon as possible so that we may consider all of them and make the best possible decision for your child's future. I enjoy very much having your child in the orchestra and look forward to talking with you.

Sincerely,

Orchestra Teacher

DATELINE: Helping parents encourage students to practice

Dear Parents:

As adults, we understand that progress and achievement are the results of effort. Students need to learn this important principle as well, and it will help them throughout their lives. Helping string students to practice on a regular basis at home will not only help them become better musicians, but better citizens as well.

Students need continued encouragement to practice, because practicing takes discipline and effort. Help your child establish a regular time and place for practicing that works in your family's schedule. Monitor your child's practice on a regular basis to ensure that it is getting done. Talk with your child about the need for practice, and set up mutually agreed upon goals and rewards. The goals should be clear and attainable. The rewards should be something valuable and enjoyable to the child.

Frequently ask your child to perform for you, demonstrating the skills, knowledge, and new music learned while practicing at home. Praise your child's practice efforts regularly in front of family members and their peers. It will make them feel good about their efforts and about themselves. It will also encourage them to continue practicing and help deepen their relationship with you.

Point out to your child the progress (he/she) has made on (his/her) instrument, and how many more notes and pieces (he/she) can now play compared to when (he/she) started, for example. Encourage your child to make up his or her own music as directed by (his/her) teacher. Help your child to remember the past successes as motivators to work toward future successes.

Practicing takes effort, and encouraging students to practice regularly takes effort. However, practice is essential for learning, and it helps develop work habits that students can take with them throughout life. Please do not hesitate to contact me for additional suggestions.

Sincerely,

Orchestra Teacher

Performance Evaluation

Name_____

SKILL	POINTS POSSIBLE	SCORE
Playing Position	10	_____
Correct Notes	20	_____
Rhythm and Tempo	10	_____
Bow Placement and Distribution	10	_____
Bowings	10	_____
Intonation	10	_____
Tone Quality	10	_____
Phrasing and Style	10	_____
Dynamics	10	_____

TOTAL _____

GRADE _____

COMMENTS:

Bowing Skills Quiz

Name_____   Date: _____

Grading Scale: 4 = Outstanding   3 = Acceptable   2 = Needs Work   1 = Poor

Right Hand

Shoulder Relaxed	4	3	2	1
Elbow Position	4	3	2	1
Wrist Position	4	3	2	1
Bow Hand Shape	4	3	2	1
Bow Parallel	4	3	2	1
String Crossing	4	3	2	1
Quality of Sound	4	3	2	1

Bowing

Shoulder Relaxed	4	3	2	1
Elbow Position	4	3	2	1
Wrist Position	4	3	2	1
Bow Parallel	4	3	2	1
Sounding Point	4	3	2	1
Overall Quality of Sound	4	3	2	1

Grading Scale: 48 – 52 = A   Points Earned _____
                    40 – 47 = B
                    30 – 39 = C   Grade _____
                    20 – 29 = D
                    10 – 19 = F

Comments _____

_____

_____

Instrument Position and Left Hand Playing Skills Quiz

Name_____

Date_____

	Points Possible	**Points Earned**
Body Position		
Feet Balanced	5	_____
Correct posture	10	_____
Shoulders Relaxed	5	_____
Instrument Position		
Elbow Position Acceptable	10	_____
Instrument Touching Body Properly	10	_____
Left Hand Position		
Fingers Curved Over Fingerboard	10	_____
Thumb Shape/Position	10	_____
Wrist Straight and Relaxed	10	_____
Correct Finger Patterns	10	_____
Intonation	20	_____

Comments _____

_____

_____

Total _____   Grade _____

Scale Test

Name_____

Date_____

	Points Possible	Points Earned
Right Hand		
Elbow and Wrist Positions	5	_____
Bow Hand Shape	10	_____
Bow Parallel	10	_____
Quality of Sound	20	_____
Left Hand		
Body Position	5	_____
Instrument Position	5	_____
Elbow Position	5	_____
Hand Shape	5	_____
Intonation	20	_____
Correct Notes	15	_____

Comment _____

_____

_____

Total _____   Grade _____

Essential Elements Quiz – Jesse James (#36)

Name_____

Date_____

	Points Possible	**Points Earned**
Bowing		
Bow Hand Shape	5	_____
Bow Parallel	15	_____
Quality of Sound	15	_____
Dynamics	10	_____
Left Hand		
Body Position	5	_____
Instrument Position	5	_____
Left Hand Shape	5	_____
Correct Pitches	10	_____
Counting Eighth Notes/Rests	15	_____
Intonation	15	_____

Comments _____

_____

_____

Total _____   Grade _____

Essential Elements Quiz – Rondeau (#47)

Name_____

Date_____

	Points Possible	**Points Earned**
Bowing		
Bow Hand Shape	10	_____
Bow Parallel	5	_____
Quality of Sound	10	_____
Left Hand		
Body Position	5	_____
Instrument Position	10	_____
Left Hand Shape	10	_____
Correct Pitches	15	_____
Dotted Quarter Rhythms	20	_____
Intonation	15	_____

Comments: _____

_____

_____

Total _____   Grade _____

A Major Scale Quiz (#55)

Name_____

Date_____

	Points Possible	**Points Earned**
Left Hand		
Body Position	10	_____
Instrument Position	10	_____
Left Hand Shape	10	_____
Forward Extension (cello)	20	_____
Extended Third Finger (violin/viola)	20	_____
Half Position (bass)	20	_____
Correct Pitches	15	_____
Intonation		
G string C♯/D string G♯	20	_____
General Intonation	15	_____

Comments _____

_____

_____

Total _____   Grade _____

You can mark your progress through the book on this page. Fill in the stars as instructed by your orchestra teacher.

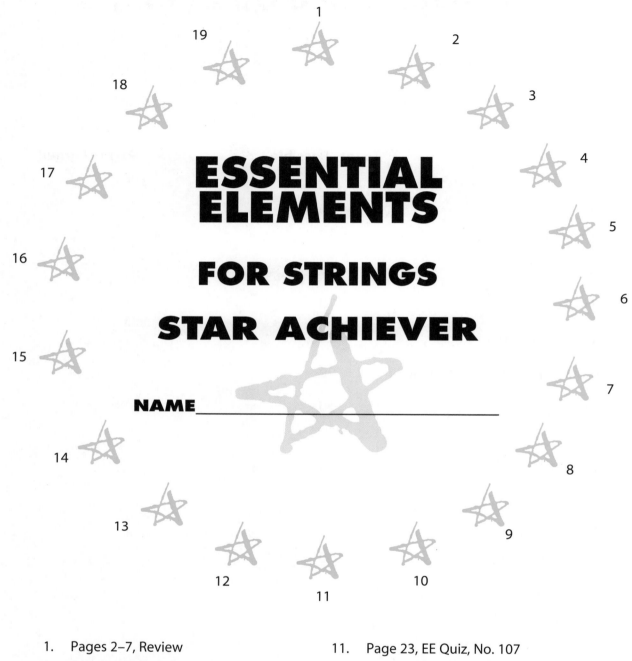

ESSENTIAL
ELEMENTS

FOR STRINGS

STAR ACHIEVER

NAME_____

1. Pages 2–7, Review
2. Page 3, *Workouts*
3. Page 8, Essential Creativity, No. 29
4. Page 9, EE Quiz, No. 36
5. Page 11, Essential Creativity, No. 44
6. Page 11, EE Quiz, No. 47
7. Page 13, EE Quiz, No. 56
8. Page 17, EE Quiz, No. 79
9. Page 18, Essential Creativity, No. 85
10. Page 19, EE Quiz, No. 91
11. Page 23, EE Quiz, No. 107
12. Page 25, Essential Creativity, No. 114
13. Page 29, EE Quiz, No. 132
14. Pages 34–37, Performance Spotlight
15. Page 38, Sight-reading
16. Page 39, Preparing for Higher Positions
17. Pages 40–43, Finger Patterns
18. Pages 44–45, Scales
19. Page 46, Creating Music

MUSIC — AN ESSENTIAL ELEMENT OF LIFE

D MAJOR

Teacher The objective of pages 2–7 is to review the fundamental playing concepts presented in *Book 1*. As students practice these pages use the following checkpoints to guide you in evaluating their performance:

1. standing or seated posture
2. instrument position
3. left hand shape
4. correct fingerings
5. bow hand shape
6. détaché stroke
   a. bow traveling parallel to the bridge
   b. string crossings
   c. slurring
7. staccato stroke and hooked bowing
8. rhythm reading accuracy
9. counting
10. note reading accuracy
11. intonation accuracy

Tone Production Principles

When evaluating your students' tone production when they are playing individually and in groups, remind them that generally cello and especially bass players should pull their bows slower than violin and viola players. In addition, be sure to tell students in which part of the bow they should play: lower half, middle, or upper half. Your decision should be based on many factors, including the style, tempo, and dynamics of the music. To assist students in understanding tone production, allow individual students to play simple melodies. Then ask students to describe the important characteristics of an acceptable sound. This can be done individually or in small groups. Ask students to describe the different characteristics of sound produced by the various sections in the orchestra.

Teacher The objectives of student book page 2 are to review the key of D Major, $\frac{4}{4}$ time signature, two-note slurs, whole, half, and quarter notes. New concepts presented include the definition of a major scale and legato style.

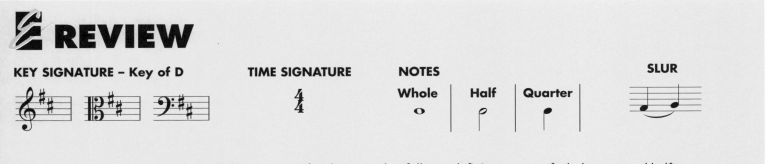

REVIEW

KEY SIGNATURE – Key of D

TIME SIGNATURE

NOTES
Whole Half Quarter

SLUR

Major Scale   A Major Scale is a series of eight notes that follow a definite pattern of whole steps and half steps. Half steps appear only between scale steps 3–4 and 7–8. Every major scale has the same arrangement of whole steps and half steps.

D MAJOR

Teacher   Begin each class with tuning the open strings. Strategies for tuning strings in an orchestra appear on page 290 in the back of the *Teacher's Manual*. Tune to the open string pitches on track one of the *Play-Along CD* if you are planning to use the CD in your teaching. In that way your students' strings will be the same pitch as those on the CD.

1. TUNING TRACK

Teacher   The circled numbers above the staff in *2. D Major Scale – Round,* indicate staggered entrances for playing the piece as a round. Discuss the definition of a major scale, emphasizing the sequence of half and whole steps. Have students create a G Major scale based on the half and whole step sequence found in the D Major scale.

Bass   The basses are required to shift from first position to third and back. Shifting for basses was introduced in *Book 1* on student book page 11 (*Teacher's Manual* page 73). To review, be sure bass players release their hand weight on the string before and during the shift, and that the thumb and hand move together as a unit. Also check that students arrive in the new position with a good left-hand shape.

Dashes before finger numbers are used to indicate both ascending and descending shifts. The following positions are used in this book and are indicated in the student books by Roman numerals:

1/2   =   Half position (first finger plays G♯ on the G string)

I   =   First position (first finger plays A on the G string)

II   =   Second position (first finger plays B♭ on the G string)

II 1/2 =   Second and a half position (first finger plays B on the G string)

III   =   Third position (first finger plays C on the G string)

2. D MAJOR SCALE – Round *(When group A reaches ②, group B begins at ①)*

D MAJOR

Teacher Constantly check the accuracy of your students' intonation. Young string players can play in tune. Normally they will play in tune only as well as the teacher requires. Maintain a high standard of intonation with your students and it will benefit them in all of their future playing.

3. D MAJOR ARPEGGIO   1/13/2022

Bass Basses shift to II 1/2 position for the first time in measure five of *D Major Mania*. Review this with basses until they have mastered this shift, since it will appear throughout the book. Fourth fingers for violin and viola are marked when phrases stay on one string. When string crossings are involved use your own discretion in determining when your student should use 4th fingers.

4. D MAJOR MANIA 1/13/2022

D MAJOR

Legato   Play in a smooth and connected style.

Teacher   Discuss the definition of the term *Legato*. Demonstrate legato bowing and contrast it with staccato bowing. Be sure students play *Theme from London Symphony* with a legato bow stroke. Review the life and contributions of Franz Haydn. His *Surprise Symphony Theme* was introduced in *Book 1* on student book page 42 (*Teacher's Manual* page 230).

5. THEME FROM LONDON SYMPHONY   1/27/22

Franz J. Haydn (1732–1809)

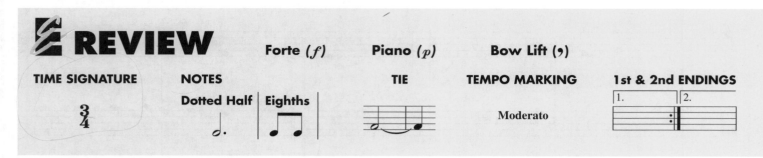

REVIEW — Forte (*f*)   Piano (*p*)   Bow Lift (,)

TIME SIGNATURE	NOTES		TIE	TEMPO MARKING	1st & 2nd ENDINGS
¾	Dotted Half	Eighths		Moderato	

3/4 RHYTHMS

Teacher The objectives of student book page 3 are to review ¾ meter, dotted half and eighth notes, ties, 1st & 2nd endings, *forte* and *piano* dynamics, bow lifts, and *moderato* tempo marking. New concepts presented include *crescendo* and *decrescendo* dynamics, plus rote practice exercises for shaping the left hand and preparing for shifting.

6. D MAJOR IN THREES   1/27/22

Teacher   Instruct students about the three variables involved in sound production on string instruments: bow speed, weight on the bow, and the location of the bow on the string (sounding point, or contact point). Demonstrate and discuss how these three variables work independently and may be combined to produce different sounds on their instruments. Have students first experiment with different combinations of the variables to produce crescendo and decrescendo dynamic changes on open strings and then while playing simple scales.

Be sure that students understand that they can play louder or softer on their instruments by manipulating all three variables, not just by changing the weight on the bow. Show them how increasing their bow speed, or moving their bow closer to the bridge, also produces more sound.

Dynamics	crescendo (*cresc.*) decrescendo (*decresc.*)		Gradually increase volume. Gradually decrease volume.

Teacher   To help students prepare for *Dynamic Contrasts,* remind them to use a slow bow for dotted half notes. Also, have students tune the first note D to their open D string that sounds an octave lower.

7. DYNAMIC CONTRASTS

HISTORY

Norwegian composer **Edvard Grieg** wrote *Peer Gynt Suite* for a play by Henrik Ibsen in 1875, the year before the telephone was invented by Alexander Graham Bell. "Morning" is a melody from *Peer Gynt Suite*. Music used in plays, or in films and television, is called **incidental music**.

Teacher   Present the life and contributions of Edvard Grieg. Play a professional recording of his *Peer Gynt Suite* from which *Morning from Peer Gynt* is excerpted. Discuss the concept of incidental music and give examples, e.g. song tracks from movie music.

8. MORNING (from Peer Gynt)

2-10-22

Edvard Grieg (1843–1907)

Teacher Discuss the life and contributions of Jacques Offenbach, composer of the melody in *Barcarolle*. Information about Offenbach, composer of the famous melody *Can-Can*, was first presented in *Book 1*, student book page 25 (*Teacher's Manual* page 136).

9. BARCAROLLE

Jacques Offenbach (1819–1880)

Teacher   The objective of the *Workouts* presented on student page 3, is to provide rote exercises for students to practice refining their left hand shapes, relax their left hand, and prepare for shifting and vibrato. Students should practice their *Workouts* frequently for review and mastery of these important skills. Violin and violas should bring their arm and hand around the instrument when sliding to higher positions, and cellos and basses should raise their left arm as they prepare to shift to higher positions.

Tunneling: Have students practice sliding all four fingers up and down the length of the fingerboard between any two adjacent strings. Then have students slide their fourth finger, third finger, and third and fourth finger together to help shape their left hand while sliding.

Ridin' The Rails: This strategy is the same as *Tunneling,* but students should slide their fingers on one string. Encourage students to slide their fingers lightly on top of the string and to be sure to keep their fingers on the string while sliding.

Tappin' And Slidin': Have students lightly tap their fingers up and down on a string before sliding to a new position. After arriving at the new position, have students lightly tap their fingers on the string again. Eventually students may use different fingers on other strings while tapping and sliding to help relax across-the-string finger patterns.

Violin/Viola

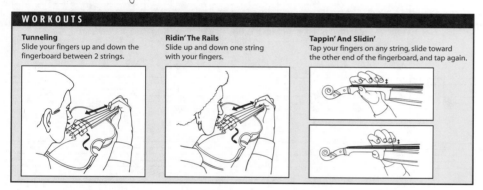

Cello

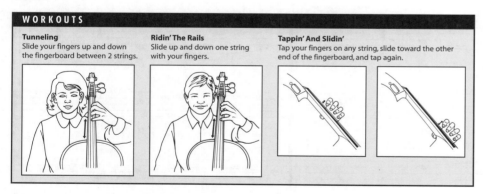

Bass

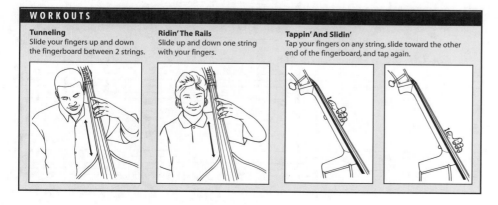

Teacher The objectives of student book page 4 are to review the key of G Major, hooked bowing, and the tempo marking *Andante.* New concepts presented include identifying intervals.

REVIEW

KEY SIGNATURE – Key of G

HOOKED BOWING

TEMPO MARKING

Andante

Teacher In *10. G Major Scale,* students can check their intonation against different sections of the orchestra. Also, one section of the orchestra may play open G strings continuously throughout the round to help other sections tune their G scale. The circled numbers above the staff indicate staggered entrances for playing the piece as a round.

10. G MAJOR SCALE – Round 2/17/22

G MAJOR

Teacher Review the definition of *arpeggio* and have students practice pronouncing and spelling it.

11. G MAJOR ARPEGGIO

Interval

The distance between two notes is called an interval. Start with "1" on the lower note, and count each line and space between the notes. The number of the higher note is the distance, or name, of the interval.

Teacher   The concept of intervals is presented to help students understand the distance between pitches. For homework assignments consider having students mark the intervals in music they have previously learned.

12. SCALE INTERVALS

G MAJOR

Teacher   Discuss the life and times of the composer William Billings (1746–1800). His melody in *Chester* contains both legato and hooked bowing. Point out to students that Billings is considered one of the first American composers who wrote in classical style, similar to the music of European composers of the time.

13. CHESTER

William Billings (1746–1800)

Is your left hand shaped properly?

Teacher   At the bottom of student book page 4 there is a check, requesting that students evaluate their left-hand shape. These **EE Checks** appear throughout the book. They are special reminders for students to evaluate the playing skills that have just been introduced. It also assists students in learning to evaluate their own skills. Self-evaluation should be encouraged to help students develop musical independence.

G MAJOR

Teacher The objectives of student book page 5 are to review the upper octave of the G Major scale (violin) and the tempo marking *Allegro*.

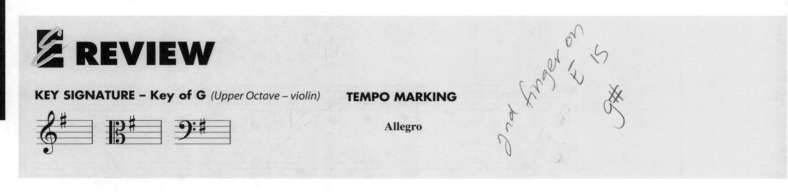

REVIEW

KEY SIGNATURE – Key of G *(Upper Octave – violin)*   **TEMPO MARKING**

Allegro

[handwritten: 2nd finger on G or E is G#]

Violin Remind violin students that the 1-2 (first and second fingers touching) pattern is used to play the upper octave G Major scale.

14. G MAJOR SCALE *(Upper Octave – violin)*

[handwritten: 3/10/22]

G MAJOR

Emi   Bmi   C   Gsus   G   C/D   G/D   Dsus   Gsus   G

15. G MAJOR ARPEGGIO *(Upper Octave – violin)*

G7   C7   A7   D7   G7

G MAJOR

Intonation
Intonation is how well each note is played in tune.

Teacher   The definition of intonation is presented on student book page 5. Exercise *16. Intonation Encounter*, is designed so students can listen and tune their playing with other sections of the orchestra in the key of G Major. Be sure to maintain a high standard of intonation for your students, because the foundation for all of their future playing is now being developed.

16. INTONATION ENCOUNTER – Duet

17. THE OUTBACK

C MAJOR

Teacher   The objectives of student book page 6 are to review the key of C Major, $\frac{2}{4}$ time, and staccato bowing.

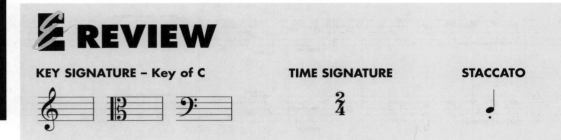

REVIEW

KEY SIGNATURE – Key of C	TIME SIGNATURE	STACCATO

Teacher   Contrast the *C Major Scale* and the *C Major Arpeggio* with exercises 14 and 15 in G Major. Have students create a D Major version so that they can quickly review all three keys.

18. C MAJOR SCALE

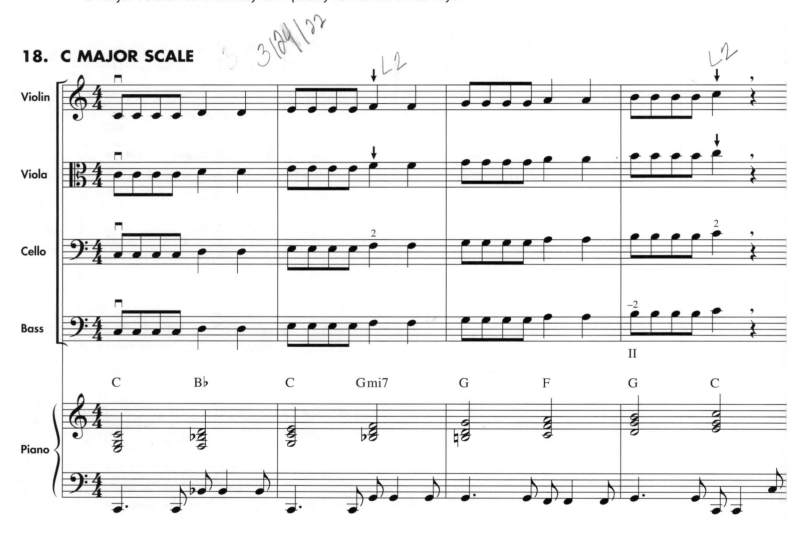

19. C MAJOR ARPEGGIO 3/24/22

C MAJOR

20. C MAJOR DUET

Teacher To prepare students for *Buffalo Gals,* discuss the tempo marking *Allegretto.* Contrast it with the tempos of *Andante* and *Allegro.* Play *Buffalo Gals* at *Andante, Allegro,* and *Allegretto* to increase students' understanding of these tempos. Also, remind students of the sudden dynamic changes in measures 5 and 9. Review with them what they should do with their bows to produce the changes. Also check to see if the students play measure 14 staccato.

21. BUFFALO GALS

Cool White (John Hodges)

Allegretto ◁ *A lively tempo, faster than **Andante**, but slower than **Allegro**.*

Check your bow hand. Are your fingers curved and is your thumb bent?

C MAJOR

Teacher   The objectives of student book page 7 are to review the lower octave C Major scale for viola and cello, and to review basic principles for tone production on string instruments. *Mezzo piano* and *mezzo forte* dynamics also are presented.

 **REVIEW**

KEY SIGNATURE – Key of C *(Lower Octave – viola, cello)*   **TIME SIGNATURE**   **TONE PRODUCTION**

- place bow between bridge and fingerboard
- bow straight
- proper weight

Teacher   After teaching *C Major Scale – Round* and *C Major Arpeggio,* have viola and cello students add the upper octave C Major scale that they already know to create a two-octave scale.

22. C MAJOR SCALE – Round   *(Lower Octave – viola and cello)*

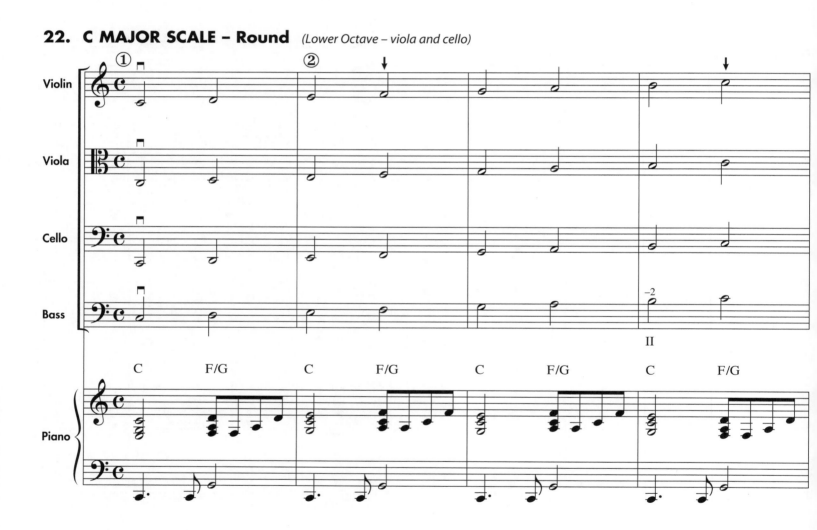

23. C MAJOR ARPEGGIO *(Lower Octave – viola and cello)*

C MAJOR

24. C MAJOR MANIA

Dynamics
mp (mezzo piano) Play moderately soft.
mf (mezzo forte) Play moderately loud.

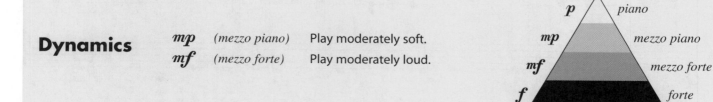

C MAJOR

Teacher To prepare students for *Crossroads,* show students the continuum of dynamics between *forte* and *piano* as indicated in the diagram. Note there is a *decrescendo* in the last two measures.

Have students practice combining the three sound production variables of bow speed, weight, and location of the bow on open strings to produce four different dynamic levels: *forte, mezzo forte, mezzo piano,* and *piano.* Also, write out a simple review scale for students indicating different dynamic levels. Have students practice changing dynamic levels as they play the scale.

25. CROSSROADS

3/31/22 ✓

CHANGING BOW SPEED

Change the bow speed according to the length of the note. When you have a longer note value, the bow speed should be slower.
If there is a dotted half note on a down bow and a quarter note on an up bow, the speed of the bow must change.

Example:

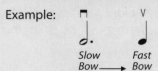

Slow Bow ⟶ *Fast Bow*

Teacher The skill of changing bow speed is reviewed on student book page 8. It was first presented in *Book 1* on student
book page 22 (*Teacher's Manual* page 120). To help students prepare for *26. The Dot Always Counts,* remind them
to slow down their bow speed for dotted half notes, compared to faster bow speeds needed for quarter notes.

26. THE DOT ALWAYS COUNTS

27. ALOUETTE

French Folk Song

Teacher Discuss the life and times of the great English composer, Henry Purcell (1659–1695), the composer of the melody *Riguadon*. Purcell was a singer and organist who became one of the most famous composers in the 17th century in England. He composed music for many plays that were performed in schools throughout England, including his famous opera *Dido and Aeneas* in 1689. While Purcell was composing his music in England, New Amsterdam became New York (1664), and Philadelphia was founded by William Penn (1682).

28. RIGAUDON

Henry Purcell (1659–1695)

RHYTHMS

Teacher Exercise *29. Essential Creativity – Oh! Susannah,* gives students the opportunity to be creative by choosing their own dynamics and writing them in the music. Give students opportunities to perform their melodies with the dynamics they have chosen. Have them describe the sounds that different dynamics create. Students may choose from *forte, piano, mezzo piano, mezzo forte, decrescendo* and *crescendo* dynamics. Refer students to the dynamic graphic on student book page 7 if they need assistance.

The words to *Oh! Susannah* are provided in the back of the *Teacher's Manual,* page 289. Feel free to make copies of the words for your students to sing. Students can sing the melody while you accompany them on the piano or while listening to the Play Along Trax accompaniment. This helps them learn what the melody should sound like, allowing the ear to lead the hand. Research suggests that students can learn more efficiently if their aural skills are well developed, aiding them in pitch memory, intonation, and pitch recognition.

Discuss the life and times of Stephen Foster (1826–1864). Foster is considered one of the first great American songwriters. He wrote many songs about early American, including *Beautiful Dreamer, My Old Kentucky Home,* and *Massa's in De Cold, Cold Ground.*

29. ESSENTIAL CREATIVITY – OH! SUSANNAH

Make up your own dynamics and write them in the music. Play the line and describe how the dynamics change the sound.

Stephen C. Foster (1826–1864)

Eighth Note & Eighth Rest

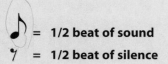

♪ = 1/2 beat of sound
𝄾 = 1/2 beat of silence

RHYTHMS

Teacher The objectives of student book page 9 are to review eighth notes and introduce eighth rests. *Rhythm Raps* are used to introduce new rhythms and meters to the string class. The exercises immediately following each *Rhythm Rap* are in the same rhythm to help students combine their bowing, fingering, and rhythm reading skills. The following is a six-step practice routine to help students learn Rhythm Raps while tapping their toes on the pulse:

Step 1 – Sing on any syllable.

Step 2 – Play pizzicato on any pitch.

Step 3 – Bow rhythm in the air vertically or through a tube.

Step 4 – Bow rhythm on any open string.

Step 5 – Bow rhythm on a scale.

Step 6 – Play with the Play-Along Trax

Eighth rests are introduced in *30. Rhythm Rap.* Eighth notes were first introduced in *Book 1,* on page 20. Have students follow the practice routine above, or one that you design, as they play in class and practice at home.

30. RHYTHM RAP ♪𝄾 *Shadow bow and count before playing.*

Teacher Point out to students that the rhythm in *31. Eighth Notes On the Beat,* is the same rhythm they have been practicing in *30. Rhythm Rap.*

31. EIGHTH NOTES ON THE BEAT 4/7/22

Teacher Show and explain to students that in *Short And Sweet,* the length of the staccato notes should be the same as the combinations of eighth notes and eighth rests.

32. SHORT AND SWEET 4/7/22

Student books have repeats, not 1st and 2nd endings.

Teacher Compare and contrast for students the rhythms in *30. Rhythm Rap,* and *33. Rhythm Rap.* Be sure students are counting and tapping as they are learning to play the rhythms. Most teachers use the 1 & 2 & counting system with their students and it appears throughout this series. However, other systems may be used to teach students to count, such as the Eastman counting system (web site: http://utminers.utep.edu/mfountai/Eastman2.htm) or the system developed by Edwin Gordon. Use whatever system you prefer. Teaching string students to count is critica to their rhythmical understanding.

33. RHYTHM RAP *Shadow bow and count before playing.*

34. EIGHTH NOTES OFF THE BEAT

35. SUNNY DAY

4/14/22

RHYTHMS

Teacher   The learning objectives of each quiz are listed. Objectives highlight the exact elements being reviewed and tested. Review exercises suggest specific examples for students requiring additional practice. Be certain students meet your performance expectations on every quiz.

QUIZ OBJECTIVES – JESSE JAMES
- *mf* dynamics
- crescendo and decrescendo
- eighth note
- eighth rest

Review Exercises:
   28. Rigaudon
   31. Eighth Notes On the Beat
   34. Eighth Notes Off the Beat
   35. Sunny Day

Teacher   While students are learning exercise 36. discuss the life and times of Jesse James (1847–1882). James was an outlaw and gunslinger. He made his living by robbing banks and trains throughout Missouri and Kansas. *Exercise 36* is an American folk song about this Robin Hood legend who helped the poor. During his lifetime, French impressionistic painters Edouard Manet and Claude Monet created some of their most famous paintings, author Herman Melville wrote *Moby Dick,* and Lewis Carroll wrote *Alice in Wonderland.*

36. ESSENTIAL ELEMENTS QUIZ – JESSE JAMES

Folk Ballad from Missouri

Teacher　The objectives of student book page 10 are to introduce the dotted quarter note followed by an eighth note rhythm, and the concept of a fermata.

Teacher　*37. Rhythm Rap,* introduces to students the rhythm of a dotted quarter note followed by an eighth note. Demonstrate this rhythm for them and use the practice suggestions, or your own ideas, for teaching. Be sure to practice this line on open strings with only one pitch per measure, before having students attempt *The Dot Counts.* In your instructions, point out and demonstrate to students that a quarter note tied to an eighth note sounds the same as a dotted quarter note. Also show students that the eighth note following the tied quarter-eighth notes must be played with a fast bow, as should the eighth note following the dotted quarter note.

37. RHYTHM RAP　*Shadow bow and count before playing.*

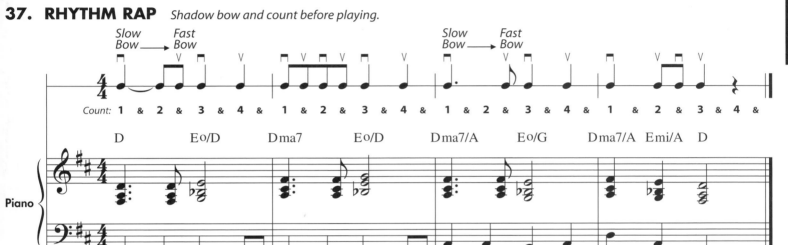

Teacher　Be sure students understand and can demonstrate correct counting while playing *The Dot Counts.*

38. THE DOT COUNTS

39. WATCH THE DOT

Student books have repeats, not 1st and 2nd endings.

40. D MAJOR SEQUENCE

41. DOTS ON THE MOVE

Teacher Define and demonstrate *fermata*. Explain to students that they must always slow their bow speed so that the fermata pitch can be sustained as long as the teacher asks. Have them experiment with different bow speeds using a "miles per hour" analogy: the slower the bow speed needed, the slower the miles per hour (i.e., 20 miles per hour bows versus 65 miles per hour bows). Tell students to carefully watch the conductor so they know when the fermata ends. Divide the class into two sections: one section should play part A and one part B. Be sure that students count, and that part A is synchronized with the eighth note pulse in part B.

Fermata Hold the note (or rest) longer than normal.

Teacher   In this duet, the A & B parts are the same for all instruments.

42.   D MAJOR BONANZA – Duet

Teacher The objectives of student book page 11 are to reinforce the dotted quarter note followed by an eighth note rhythm, both single and hooked bowing, and to introduce the term *ritardando.*

43. A CAPITAL SHIP

American Folk Song

Teacher   In *44. Essential Creativity,* students are asked to add eighth note flags and dots to some of the quarter note rhythms. Give students the opportunity to play their newly created rhythms for the class. This gives you the opportunity to assess their understanding of the rhythm.

44. ESSENTIAL CREATIVITY

Create your own rhythms by penciling in a dot and a flag to change any two quarter notes from ♩ ♩ to ♩. ♪

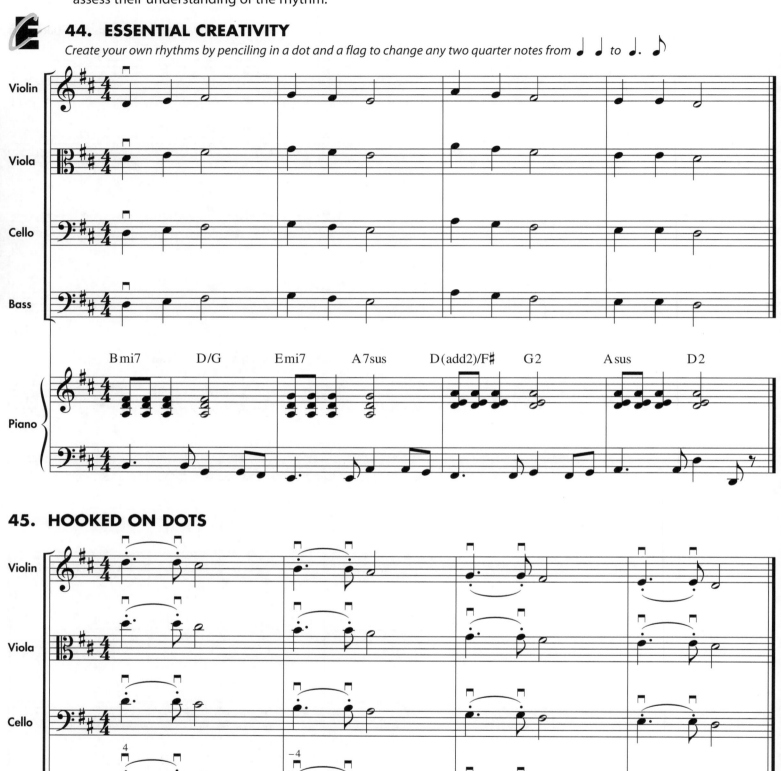

45. HOOKED ON DOTS

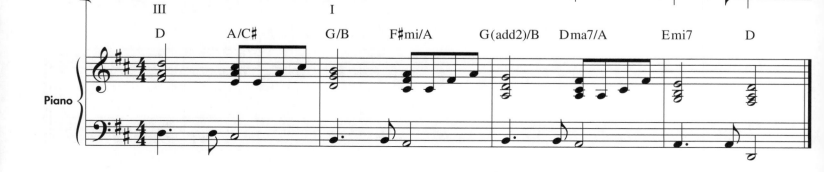

Ritardando   *ritard.* (or) *rit.* – Gradually slower

Teacher   Explain to students the meaning of the term *ritardando.* Remind students to slow their bow down during ritards and to watch their teacher when he/she is conducting. That way they will know when to play the next note or to stop playing after a *ritard.* The term *Lento* is also introduced in *Theme from New World Symphony.*

46. THEME FROM NEW WORLD SYMPHONY

Lento ◁ *Very slow tempo*

Antonin Dvořák (1841–1904)

QUIZ OBJECTIVES – RONDEAU
- Dotted quarter-eighth rhythm
- Hooked bowing
- Ritardando

Review Exercises:

RHYTHMS

47. ESSENTIAL ELEMENTS QUIZ – RONDEAU

Andantino ◁ *A tempo that is slightly quicker than* **Andante**.

Jean-Joseph Mouret (1682–1738)

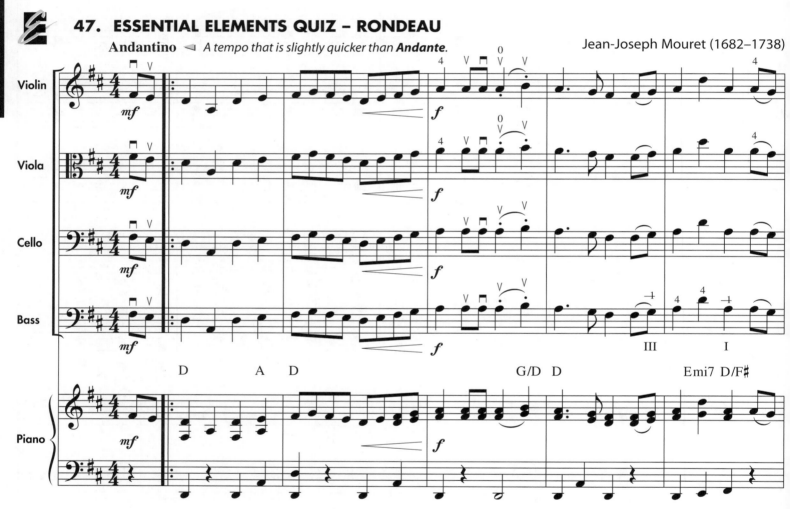

RHYTHMS

SHARP KEYS

Teacher   The objectives of student book pages 12 and 13 are to introduce the notes C♯ on the G string and G♯ on the D string. These notes require an extended third finger pattern on the violin and viola, an extended hand position on the cello, and half position for the bass.

Violin/   On student book page 12, a new finger pattern is introduced: high third finger for violin and viola for the pitch
Viola   C♯ on the G string. Have students read and follow carefully steps one and two as described in their books. Be sure to check students' left hand position to ensure that they are using the correct finger pattern and playing the C♯ in tune. Check also that their elbow comes more underneath the instrument as they play the C♯.

Violin

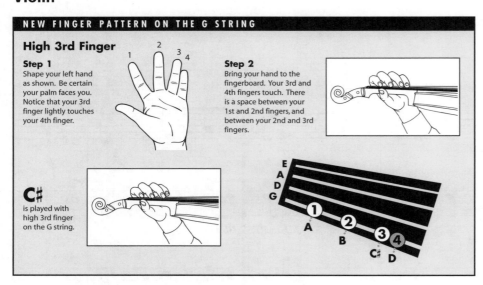

Viola

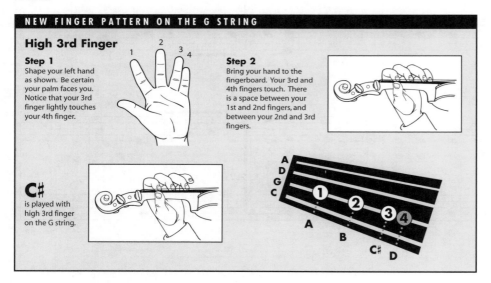

Cello   On student book page 12, forward extensions are introduced to enable cello students to play C♯ on the G string. Cellists should open their hand between the first and second fingers so that there is a whole step between these fingers. Students should move their second, third, and fourth fingers, and thumb, toward the bridge while keeping their first finger on the string. The thumb should move with the hand to remain behind the second finger in this new position. As a part of the extension, the elbow should move forward at the same time. This helps the second finger extend so that there is a whole step between the first and second fingers, particularly for those students with small hands.

Have the students extend between their first and second fingers so that their fourth finger can play C♯ to begin *Let's Read* "C♯" *(C-sharp)*. Students will be tempted to reach for the C♯ by extending the fourth finger only. Be sure that your students learn to extend correctly. It is one of the most critical skills in cello performance. Incorrect extensions are one of the most common faults of young cellists.

The following are checkpoints to help you evaluate your student cellists when they are extending forward:

- hand opens between first and second fingers
- there is a whole step between first and second fingers
- thumb moves with the hand, positioned behind the second finger
- first finger contact on the string remains the same, but the finger rests more on its side in extended position and straightens out slightly
- elbow moves toward the floor and instrument
- the fourth finger is curved

Teaching cellists to extend will require time and much reinforcement. All exercises and melodies on pages 12–15 require forward extensions and are provided to help your cellists begin to master this important skill.

In this book, X2 is used to remind students that an extension should always occur between the first and second fingers; (X)4 is used to indicate that a note with the fourth finger should be played in extended position.

Cello

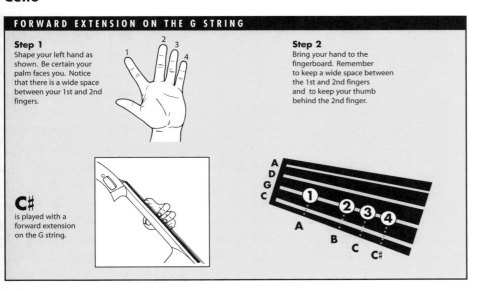

Bass

Bass A special writing exercise is provided on student book page 12 for basses while violins, violas, and cellos learn their new notes.

Bass

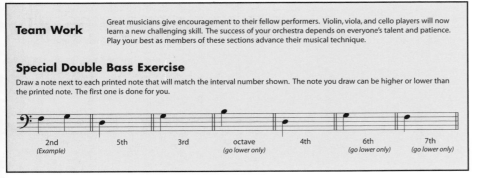

SHARP KEYS

Teacher *Listening Skills* are included every time a new note is introduced. Research suggests that students with well-developed listening skills have better left/right hand coordination, intonation, and memorization skills.

The following echo patterns are suggestions to be played behind the class to train students' ears to recognize and play C♯ in tune. To prepare students to play C♯, model it, allow the class to match the pitch while sustaining it, and then give each student the opportunity to play it individually so that his/her intonation may be evaluated. Stand behind the cello section of the orchestra when playing these echo patterns so that you can check to see that the students are moving their thumb with their hand when extending.

Listening Skills   Play what your teacher plays. Listen carefully.

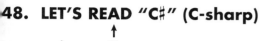

48. LET'S READ "C♯" (C-sharp)

49. STAY SHARP

50. AT PIERROT'S DOOR

French Folk Song

Student books have repeats, not 1st and 2nd endings.

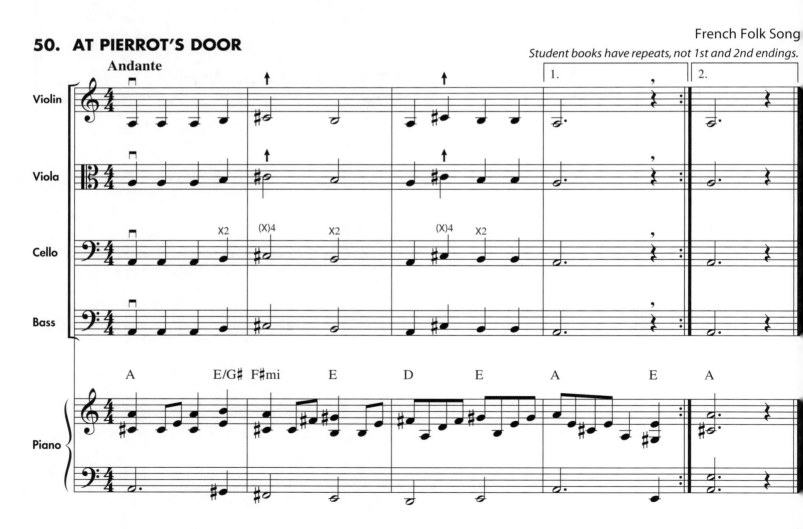

Teacher Be sure students place their fingers on the pitches B and A in the first measure of *Hot Cross Buns,* before starting the piece. Cellos should begin in extended position. This will help them play in tune and reinforce their extended finger pattern. Remind them that in extended position a B is played with the second finger.

51. HOT CROSS BUNS

Were your C♯'s in tune?

SHARP KEYS

Violin/ Viola   The high third finger introduced on page 12 is now transferred to the D string for G♯. Have students read and follow carefully steps one and two as described in their books on page 12 to help them find the G♯ on the D string. Be sure to check students' left hand position to ensure that they are using the correct fingerings and playing the G♯ in tune. They will be tempted to play the pitch flat.

Violin

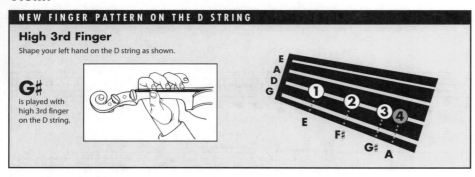

Viola

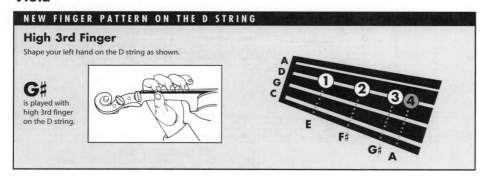

Cello   Cellos must extend for G♯ on the D string the same way they did for C♯ on the G string (student book page 12). Students should extend their second finger so that there is a whole step between their first and second fingers. This enables the fourth finger to sound G♯ as described on student book page 12. Review the teacher notes and checkpoints for cello extensions on *Teacher's Manual* page 83.

Cello

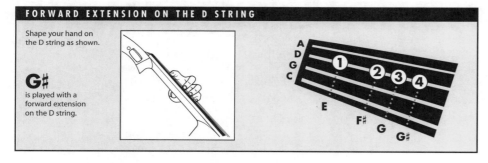

Bass   G♯ in half position on the G string is introduced. Students should place their first finger halfway between the nut and first finger A to sound the G♯. Be sure students keep their proper hand shape while fingering the G♯, with just one finger on the string. Have them study the fingerboard graphic and see that notes in half position are played with different fingers than in first position.

Bass

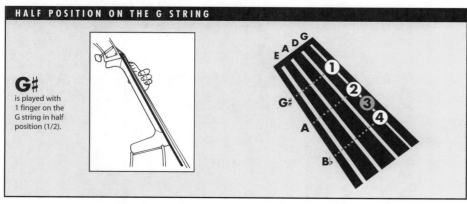

Teacher The following echo patterns are suggestions to be played behind the class to train students' ears to recognize and play G♯ in tune. To prepare students to play G♯, model it, allow the class to match the pitch while sustaining it, and then give each student the opportunity to play it individually. Check to ensure that each student's intonation is accurate. Sometimes stand behind the cello section when playing the *Listening Skills* patterns, so that you can check to see that the cellos are moving their thumbs with their second, third, and fourth fingers when extending.

Listening Skills   Play what your teacher plays. Listen carefully.

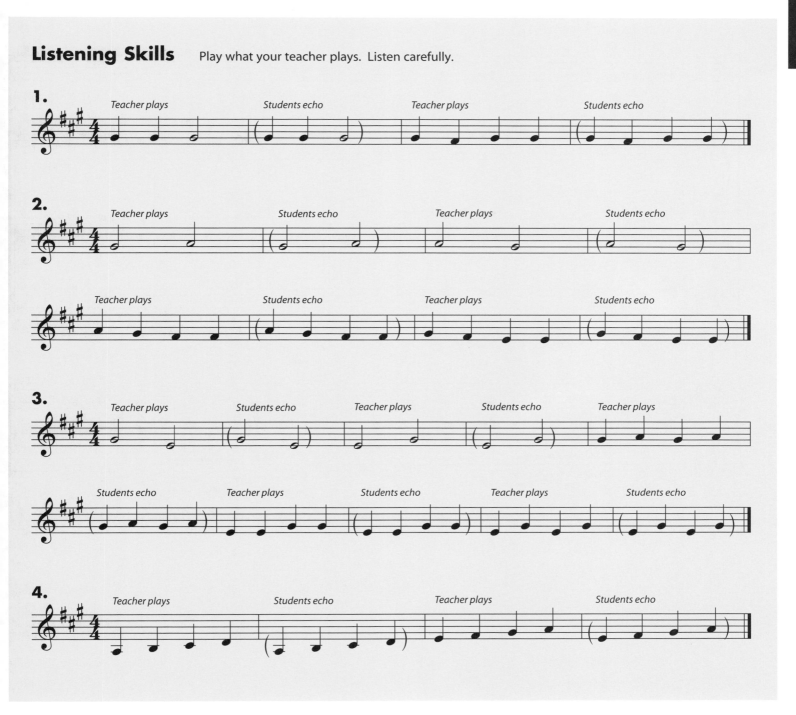

SHARP KEYS

52. LET'S READ "G♯" (G-sharp)

Violin/
Viola
Point out to students that if their third finger G# is high enough, they should be able to put their fourth finger next to it to accurately sound the pitch A. They can check their fingered A with their open A string. Also, have students transpose *Reaching Out,* to the G string, checking their fingered D with their open D string.

53. REACHING OUT

Violin/
Viola
Consider transposing *Higher And Higher,* to the G string, allowing students to reinforce the accuracy of their high third finger pattern. Be sure to have them check the fingered D with their open D string.

54. HIGHER AND HIGHER

△ *Play with 2 fingers in half position.*

SHARP KEYS

THEORY

Key Signature: A MAJOR

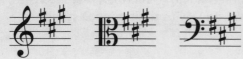

Play all F's as F♯ (F-sharp), C's as C♯ (C-sharp), and G's as G♯ (G-sharp).

Teacher   Exercise 55 introduces the A Major scale. Use many different bowing variations, and allow students to sustain each pitch so they can carefully check their finger pattern and intonation. Also point out to students the A Major key signature, which incorporates G♯. Be sure cellos are extending properly.

55. A MAJOR SCALE

QUIZ OBJECTIVES – A SONG FOR ANNE
- Key of A Major
- C# on the G string
- G# on the D string
- Forward extensions for cello
- Fourth finger on the G string for violin and viola
- Half position for bass

Review Exercises:
49. *Stay Sharp*
50. *At Pierrot's Door*
53. *Reaching Out*
55. *A Major Scale*

56. ESSENTIAL ELEMENTS QUIZ – A SONG FOR ANNE

SHARP KEYS

Violin/ While the violas and cellos learn a new F♯ on their instruments, have violin and bass players complete the
Bass   special counting exercise on student book page 14.

Violin

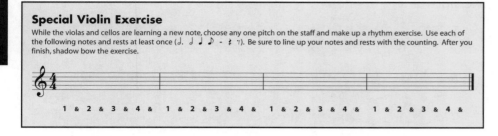

Special Violin Exercise

While the violas and cellos are learning a new note, choose any one pitch on the staff and make up a rhythm exercise. Use each of the following notes and rests at least once (♩. ♩ ♪ ♪ – ≹ ⁊). Be sure to line up your notes and rests with the counting. After you finish, shadow bow the exercise.

Bass

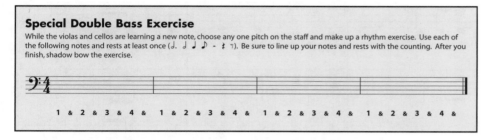

Special Double Bass Exercise

While the violas and cellos are learning a new note, choose any one pitch on the staff and make up a rhythm exercise. Use each of the following notes and rests at least once (♩. ♩ ♪ ♪ – ≹ ⁊). Be sure to line up your notes and rests with the counting. After you finish, shadow bow the exercise.

Viola/ High third finger for F♯ on the C string is introduced for viola, as well as the forward extension for F♯ on the C string
Cello   for cellos. Cellos should follow the same principles for extending on the C string as previously described for C♯ on the G string (student book page 12) and G♯ on the D string (student book page 13). Use the same guidelines listed previously for evaluating your cello students' extensions. Be sure violists move their elbow more underneath the instrument as they play the F♯ on the C string.

Viola

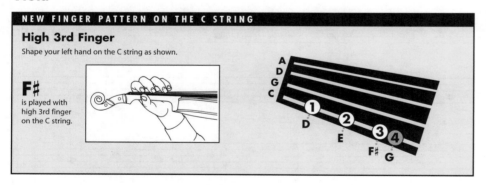

NEW FINGER PATTERN ON THE C STRING

High 3rd Finger

Shape your left hand on the C string as shown.

F♯ is played with high 3rd finger on the C string.

Cello

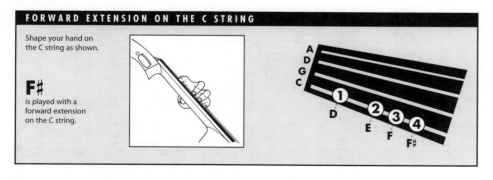

FORWARD EXTENSION ON THE C STRING

Shape your hand on the C string as shown.

F♯ is played with a forward extension on the C string.

Teacher   Play the following echo sequences, or ones you design, to train students' ears to accurately hear and play F♯. Violins can play either the F♯ on the E string or the F♯ on the D string when echoing. Occasionally play behind the cellos so that you can see if they are moving their thumbs when extending.

Listening Skills   Play what your teacher plays. Listen carefully.

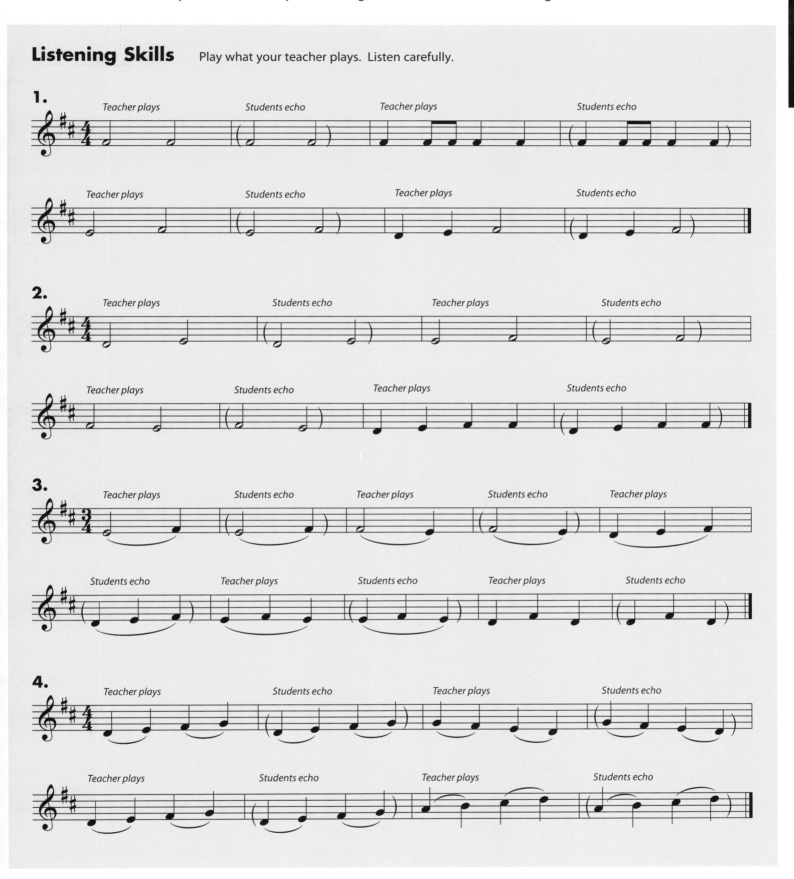

SHARP KEYS

Viola   Cello

57. LET'S READ "F♯" (F-sharp)

58. HIGH POINT

59. MAGNIFICENT MONTANA

SHARP KEYS

Teacher In *60. D Major Scale – Round,* the violas and cellos play a lower octave D Major scale beginning on the C string. The viola and cello students are now prepared to play a two-octave D Major scale on their instruments.

60. D MAJOR SCALE – Round

In the second half of the 1800s many composers tried to express the spirit of their own country by writing music with a distinct national flavor. Listen to and describe the music of Scandinavian and Spanish composers, and Russian composers such as Borodin, Tchaikovsky, and Rimsky-Korsakov. They often used folk songs and dance rhythms to convey their nationalism.

Teacher Have students discuss American patriotic songs and their use in history. Ask them to describe how American patriotic songs sound different than Russian nationlisitc songs, such as *61. Russian Folk Tune.*

61. RUSSIAN FOLK TUNE

SHARP KEYS

Teacher   The objectives of student book page 15 are to prepare the violins to play a two-octave A Major scale and to introduce G♯ on the E string for basses and violins.

A special written exercise is provided at the top of student book page 15 for violas and cellos while the violins and basses learn their new note.

Viola

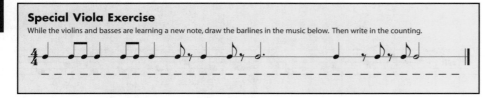

Cello

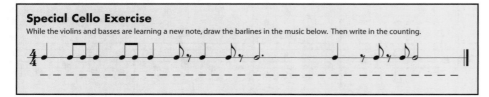

Violin   G♯ on the E string is played with a high second finger as illustrated on student book page 15. When playing any pitches on the E string, students should use a fast bow to project the sound because of the small width of the string, in addition to carefully pulling their bow parallel to the bridge.

Violin

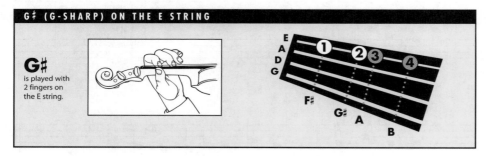

Bass   G♯ on the E string is played with four fingers in first position as illustrated on student book page 15 for the bass. When playing any pitches on the bass E string, students should pull their bow very slowly to get the best sound. The bow should travel slower on the E string than any other string on the bass.

Bass

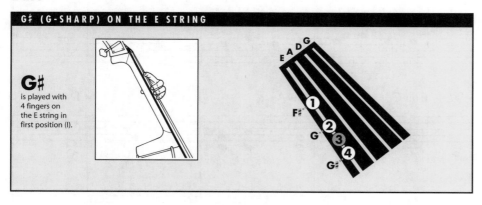

Teacher Play the following echo patterns to help students learn the sound of G♯ and discover its placement in relationship to other pitches.

Listening Skills

Play what your teacher plays. Listen carefully.

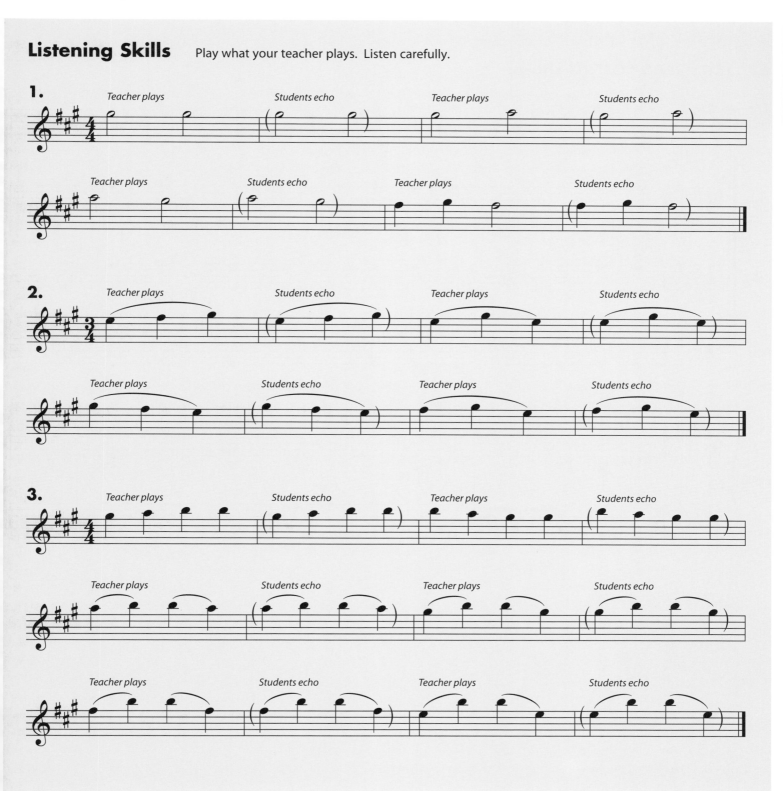

SHARP KEYS

Violin   Bass

62. LET'S READ "G♯" (G-sharp)

Teacher After students have learned to play *63. A Major Scale,* which features an upper octave of the scale, explain to them the relationship between the lower octave A Major scale that they have already learned (exercise 54, on student book page 13) and the new upper octave A Major scale in exercise 63. Have students play a two-octave A Major scale by combining exercises 55 and 63.

Teacher Consider adding many different rhythms and bowings to the scales as a part of your orchestra warm up.

63. A MAJOR SCALE

SHARP KEYS

64. A MAJOR ARPEGGIO

65. THE FIG TREE

SHARP KEYS

THEORY

Accent ♩> or >♩   Emphasize the note. Add weight or increase the speed at the beginning of the bow stroke.

Teacher The term *accent* is introduced. Explain and demonstrate to students that the most common ways to accent on string instruments are to add weight and to pull the bow faster. Practice accented strokes on open strings first. Instruct students to add weight to the bow by leaning on the bow stick with their index finger before pulling their bow to start the stroke. Accenting notes of simple scales and easy review pieces also allows students to develop their bowing skills. After students can play accented scales, begin to teach them *66. Sitka City*.

66. SITKA CITY

Moderato   Russian Folk Song

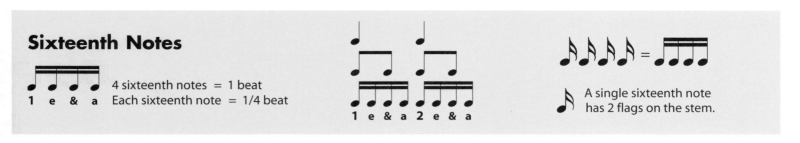

Sixteenth Notes

4 sixteenth notes = 1 beat
1 e & a   Each sixteenth note = 1/4 beat

1 e & a 2 e & a

A single sixteenth note has 2 flags on the stem.

Teacher On student book page 16, sixteenth notes are featured for the first time. Repeated sixteenth notes are first introduced on the same pitch to help students as they first learn to play and count this note value. Use the "one-e-and-a" counting system, or another one that you prefer, to help students count sixteenth notes. Be sure to explain to students the relationship between quarter, eighth, and sixteenth notes as described in the student book on the top of the page. This is an excellent opportunity to relate skills from mathematics to music. Compare fractions in math to fractions in music.

All new rhythms are first introduced in D Major, the key most familiar to students, so that it will allow students to need to learn only one new concept at a time. As students develop their reading and playing skills have them play the new rhythm in another key.

Have students count *67. Rhythm Rap*, carefully as they begin to learn sixteenth notes.

69. TECHNIQUE TRAX

RHYTHMS

70. DINAH WON'T YOU BLOW YOUR HORN

Teacher   The words to *71. Mockingbird,* by Septimus Winner are provided on page 289 for your teaching objectives. Septimus was 27 years old when he composed the *Mockingbird.* He was a music teacher and owner of a music store at the time. He also penned the tunes *Whispering Hope, Ten Little Indians,* and gave us the words to *Where Oh Where Hs My Little Dog Gone.* Alice Hawthorne was the pseudonym that Septimus used when composing the *Mockingbird.* Discuss reasons composers and authors occasionally create using pseudonyms. Pseudonyms were commonly used during the life of Septimus. For example, Mark Twain wrote under the name of Samuel Clemens.

Mockingbird sings of life in the southern United States during slavery. Discuss the Civil War and its effects on America. Also discuss the artistic developments during the life of Septimus Winner, 1827–1902.

71. MOCKINGBIRD

Alice Hawthorne (Septimus Winner) (1827–1902)

RHYTHMS

Teacher The objective of student book page 17 is to introduce two new rhythms involving sixteen notes:
Have students first clap these rhythms and then practice them on open strings as in *Rhythm Raps 72* and *75.*

72. RHYTHM RAP *Shadow bow and count before playing.*

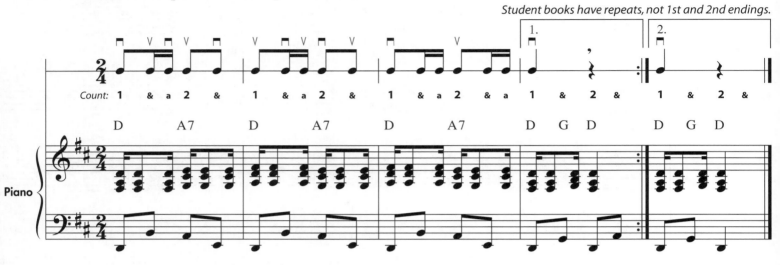

73. BLUEBERRY PIE

74. TECHNIQUE TRAX

75. RHYTHM RAP

 *Shadow bow and count before playing.*

Student books have repeats, not 1st and 2nd endings.

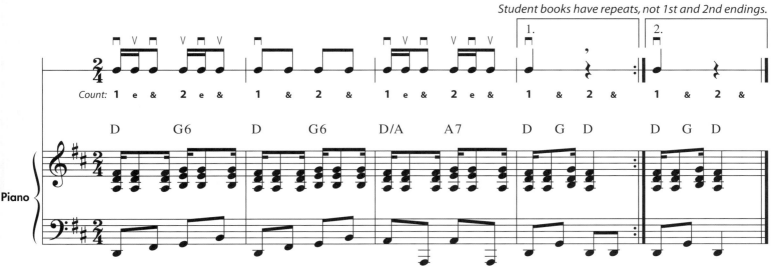

76. MARCHING ALONG

Student books have repeats, not 1st and 2nd endings.

77. ON THE MOVE

Teacher Consider dividing the orchestra into three sections while practicing *78. Rhythm Etude - Duet.* One section of the orchestra can play continuous sixteenth notes while the rest of the orchestra plays the A and B parts. This will help students keep a steady beat and understand the relationship between sixteenth, eighth, and quarter notes. Be sure students are always counting while playing.

78. RHYTHM ETUDE – Duet

QUIZ OBJECTIVES – RHYTHM ROUND-UP

- Repeated sixteenth notes
- Rhythm of an eighth and two sixteenths
- Rhythm of two sixteenths and an eighth
- Counting sixteenth notes
- Staccato eighth notes

Review Exercises:

70. *Dinah Won't You Blow Your Horn*
71. *Mockingbird*
73. *Blueberry Pie*
76. *Marching Along*

79. ESSENTIAL ELEMENTS QUIZ – RHYTHM ROUND-UP

Teacher The objective of student book page 18 is to introduce students to a dotted eighth-sixteenth rhythm with hooked bowing. Also an opportunity is given to students to write a D Major scale using any of the rhythms involving sixteenth notes that they have learned.

In *80. Rhythm Rap,* a dotted eighth note-sixteenth note rhythm with hooked bowing is introduced. Be sure students count carefully and understand that a dotted eighth note is equal to the duration of three sixteenth notes. Consider playing simple review scales using the dotted eighth note-sixteenth note rhythm to help students learn to understand and play this new rhythm.

80. RHYTHM RAP *Shadow bow and count before playing.*

Student books have repeats, not 1st and 2nd endings.

81. TECHNIQUE TRAX

Student books have repeats, not 1st and 2nd endings.

Teacher   Consider practicing *82. Hooked On D Major,* with part of the orchestra playing continuous sixteenth notes and the rest playing the printed rhythm. Students should be able to recognize that the last sixteenth note of a dotted eighth-sixteenth rhythm should line up exactly with the last sixteenth of a four sixteenth note pattern. Consider having students transpose exercise 82 to other scales, such as G, A, and C Major.

82. HOOKED ON D MAJOR

83. THE MOUNTAIN CLIMBER

84. KEEP IT SHORT

Teacher Ask students to write out a D Major scale for *85. Essential Creativity,* using any of the rhythms involving sixteenth notes they have learned on pages 16–18. Give students the opportunity to play their scales for you or the class. Assess their rhythm writing and determine if they are playing the rhythms correctly.

85. ESSENTIAL CREATIVITY

Write a D Major scale using any of the following rhythms: ♫♫, ♩♫, ♫♩, ♩.♪ *Perform your composition for the class.*

Teacher   The objective of student book page 19 is to introduce syncopation. Read the definition as presented in the student book and demonstrate sample syncopated rhythms.

Syncopation

Syncopation occurs when an accent or emphasis is given to a note that is not on a strong beat. This type of "off-beat" feel is common in many popular and classical styles.

THEORY

Teacher   The syncopated rhythm eighth-quarter-eighth is introduced in *86. Rhythm Rap.* It is very important that students learn this rhythm kinesthetically, by tapping, clapping, and counting out loud. Physical motions reinforce learning of new rhythms. When students are shadow bowing this line, be sure they continue to tap and count. Remind students to pull their bows faster on the eighth notes as compared to the quarter notes.

86. RHYTHM RAP   *Shadow bow and count before playing.*

Student books have repeats, not 1st and 2nd endings.

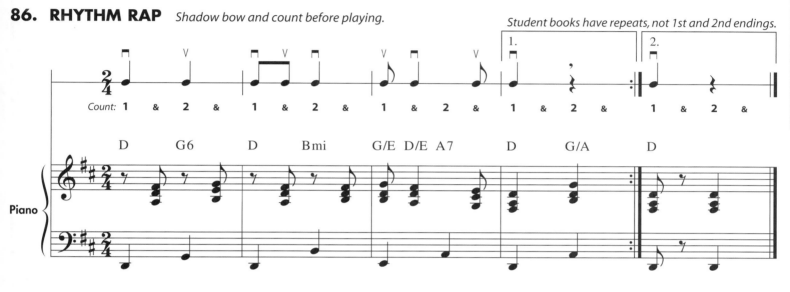

87. SYNCOPATION TIME

Student books have repeats, not 1st and 2nd endings.

RHYTHMS

Teacher   Instruct students to begin the first measure of *88. Mirror Image*, and *89. Children's Shoes*, in the upper half of the bow, so they will have enough bow for the half note in measure two. Be sure students continue counting at all times while playing.

88. MIRROR IMAGE

89. CHILDREN'S SHOES

Black American Spiritual

Teacher Hooked bowing is added to syncopated rhythms in *90. Hooked On Syncopation*. Be sure students completely stop their bows between hooked notes. Remind students to start the first measure in the middle to upper half of the bow.

90. HOOKED ON SYNCOPATION

Teacher The lyrics to the melody *Tom Dooley*, appear on page 289 in the *Teacher's Manual*. Discuss how songs can describe life's events and contribute to the culture of a region or a nation.

QUIZ OBJECTIVES – TOM DOOLEY
- Eighth-quarter-eighth syncopated rhythm
- Hooked bowing in syncopated rhythm ♪ ♩ ♪

Review Exercises:
    87. Syncopation Time
    88. Mirror Image
    89. Children's Shoes

91. ESSENTIAL ELEMENTS QUIZ – TOM DOOLEY

American Folk Song

FLAT KEYS

Violin   Student book page 20 introduces a new finger pattern, incorporating the low first finger to play B♭ on the A string. Have students read and follow carefully steps one and two as described in the student book. Be sure to check students' left hand position to ensure that they are fingering the B♭ correctly.

Violin

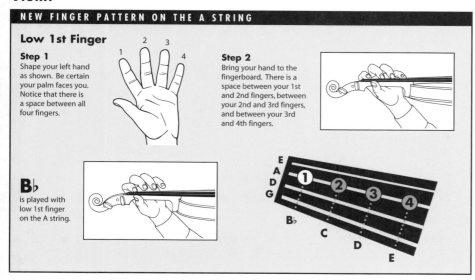

Viola/Cello   Playing B♭ on the G string requires violists and cellists to use their second finger on the G string as illustrated.

Viola

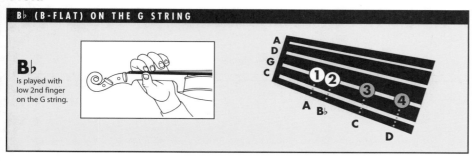

Cello

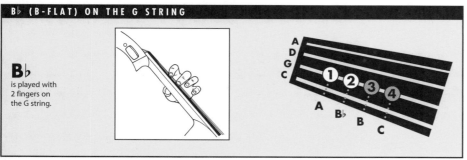

Bass   B♭ is sounded with the first finger in half position on the A string, as indicated on student book page 20. With the hand in this position review the other pitches that can be played (B♮ and C♮).

Bass

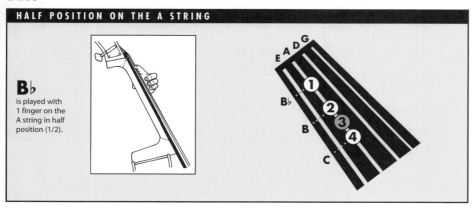

Teacher The following echo patterns are suggestions to be played behind the class to train students' ears to recognize and play B♭. Be sure to play the echo patterns behind the class so students cannot imitate your fingering. To prepare students to play B♭ in tune, model the B♭, ask the class to match the pitch and sustain it, and then give each student the opportunity to play it individually.

Listening Skills   Play what your teacher plays. Listen carefully.

92. LET'S READ "B♭" (B-flat)

93. ROLLING ALONG

Violin Be sure to encourage students to play the pitch D high enough on the first beat of measure two of *94. Matching Octaves.* Students will be tempted to play it low because it is preceded by the low first finger B♭.

94. MATCHING OCTAVES

FLAT KEYS

Violin   Student book page 21 introduces the low first finger on the E string for the pitch F♮. It is the same low first finger pattern introduced on student book page 20. Be sure to check students' left hand position to ensure that they are fingering the F♮ correctly. The key of F Major is also presented for the first time.

Violin

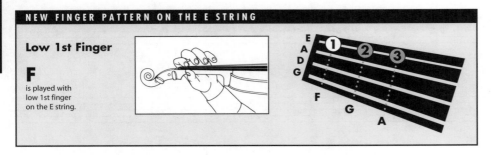

Bass   F♮ is played with the first finger in half position on the E string. With the hand in this position show the other pitches that can be played (F♯ and G♮) which are illustrated on the fingerboard diagram.

Bass

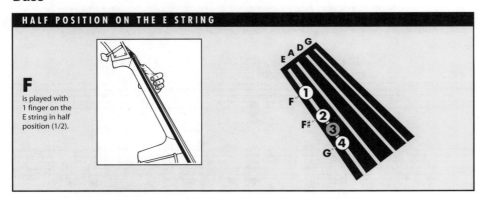

Viola/ Cello   A special writing exercise is provided for violas and cellos while the violins and the basses learn to play their new pitches.

Viola

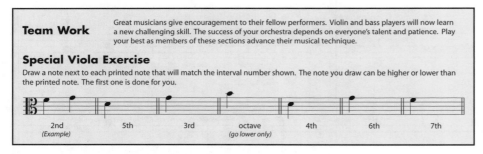

Cello

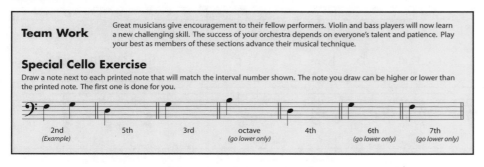

Teacher   Play the following echo patterns to help students recognize and match F♮ by ear.

Listening Skills   Play what your teacher plays. Listen carefully.

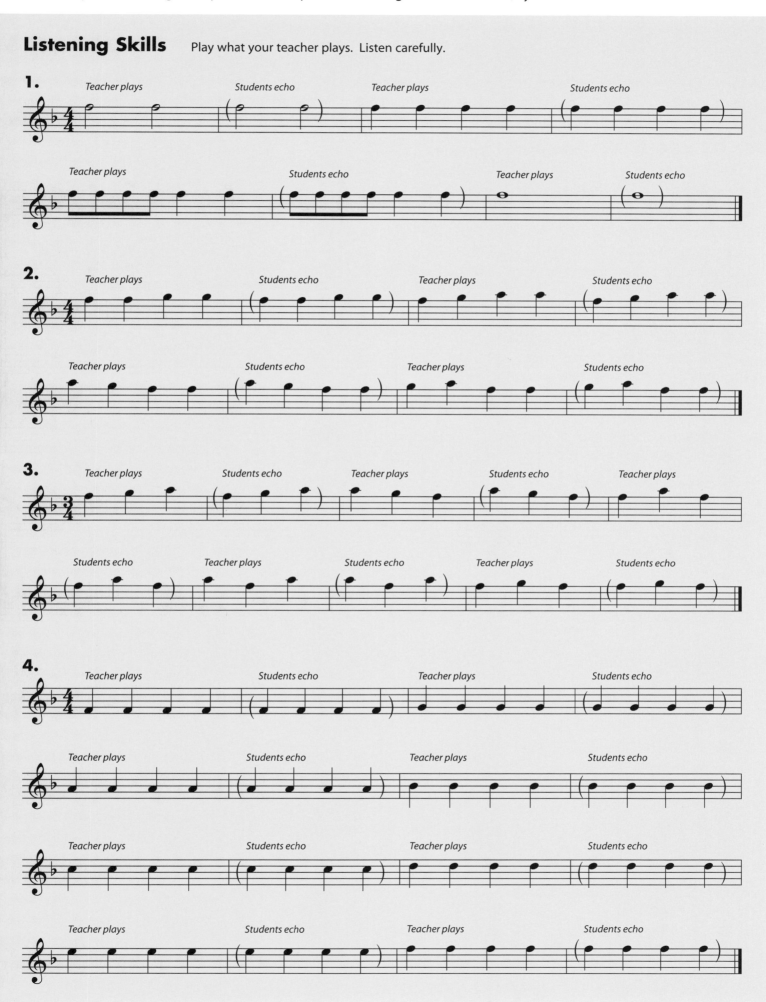

FLAT KEYS

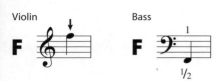

Violin   Be careful to check that G♮ and A♮ are high enough in measures three and four of exercise 95. Students will be tempted to play the pitches flat because they are preceded by the low first finger F♮.

95. LET'S READ "F" (F-natural)

Teacher Once again check carefully that there is an accurate whole step between F♮ and G♮ and between G♮ and A♮ in *Technique Trax*. Students will be tempted to make the intervals too small. Encourage them to listen carefully and spread their fingers far enough apart between the pitches so they will be in tune.

96. TECHNIQUE TRAX

FLAT KEYS

THEORY

Key Signature: F MAJOR

Play all B's as B♭ (B-flat).

Teacher To prepare students to play *97. F Major Scale,* have them first sustain each note of the F Major scale while checking their pitch accuracy carefully. Have students play the F Major scale using several different rhythms. You may demonstrate a rhythm for them and then ask them to play the scale using that rhythm. Students may also select their own rhythms for the class to play.

Discuss the F Major key signature that is introduced. Have students review the other key signatures they have learned, e.g. C, G, and D Major.

97. F MAJOR SCALE

A **Concerto** is a composition in several movements for solo instrument and orchestra. Exercise 98 is the theme from the first movement of the *Concerto for Violin and Orchestra* by **Ludwig van Beethoven**, composed while author William Wordsworth was writing his poem *I Wandered Lonely as a Cloud*. A special feature of the concerto is the *cadenza*, which was improvised, or made up, by the soloist during a concert. Improvising and creating your own music is great fun. Try it if you have not already.

Teacher Introduce the *concerto* form as defined. Play recorded examples in class. There is a commercially available videotaped performance of world-famous violinist Itzhak Perlman performing the Beethoven *Violin Concerto in D Major*. Consider obtaining it and showing it to students in class. *98. Theme from Violin Concerto* is one of the melodies from Beethoven's *Violin Concerto*.

Also, discuss with your students the concept of a cadenza and improvisation. Suggest to students that they create their own melodies. Play excerpts from recordings of Beethoven's *Violin Concerto in D Major*. As students are listening to the recordings, ask them to analyze and describe the music.

98. THEME FROM VIOLIN CONCERTO

Ludwig van Beethoven (1770–1827)

Teacher   The objective of student book page 22 is to introduce the pitches E♭ and B♭.

Violin   The low first finger for violin, previously presented on student book pages 20 and 21, is used on the D string for the pitch E♭. B♭ is played with the low second-finger pattern on the G string. A lower octave B♭ Major scale can now be played.

Viola   Low first finger on the D string for E♭ and low first finger on the A string for B♭ are introduced. This is a new finger pattern. Have students read and follow carefully steps one and two as described in the student book. Be sure to check students' left hand position to ensure that they are fingering the E♭ and B♭ correctly.

Cello   Playing E♭ on the D string and B♭ on the A string requires cellists to extend their first finger a half step backward, toward the end of the fingerboard. This backward motion is commonly called a backward extension. The first finger should be extended backward so that there is a whole step between the first and second fingers. When extending backward, the player should move the elbow and forearm forward and roll the thumb slightly on its pad, allowing the side of the first finger to contact the string. This enables the first finger to extend backward far enough to play the E♭ and B♭ in tune. Cello students must learn to extend properly, as it is a technique that is used frequently throughout cello literature. The following are checkpoints to help you evaluate your student cellists when they are extending backward:

- first finger moves a half step toward the end of the scroll
- the side of the first finger touches the string
- thumb rolls as the first finger extends backward
- elbow moves toward the floor and instrument
- there is a whole step between the first and second fingers

Teaching cellists to extend will require time and much reinforcement. Many exercises and melodies on pages 22–25 and pages 28–29 require backward extensions and are provided to help your cellists begin to master this important skill.

In this book, X1 is used to show students when a note should be played with a backward extension.

Bass   Half position is introduced on the D and G strings. E♭ is played in half position with the first finger on the D string, as shown on student book page 22. B♭ is played with four fingers on the G string. Previously learned notes will now be played with a different finger number in half position. Have students study the fingerboard graphics to determine which finger now plays each note. Be sure students keep their thumb behind their second finger in half position and all fingers poised over the string when not in use. Also check that all of their fingers are curved over the string and that they pull their bows slowly.

Teacher   Be sure violin and viola students play the E♭ low enough and are able to play the echo sequences accurately. Also check that the cello players make the backward extension for the E♭ properly. Basses should have their hands in half position.

Violin

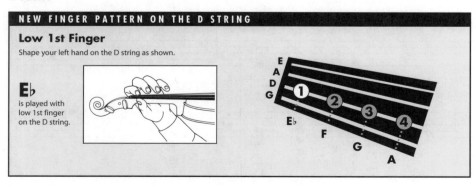

Viola

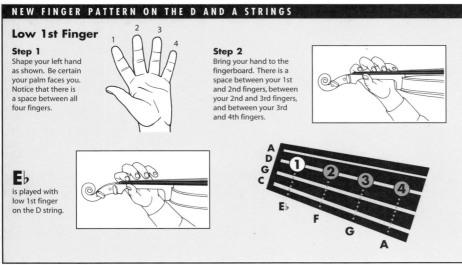

NEW FINGER PATTERN ON THE D AND A STRINGS

Low 1st Finger

Step 1
Shape your left hand as shown. Be certain your palm faces you. Notice that there is a space between all four fingers.

Step 2
Bring your hand to the fingerboard. There is a space between your 1st and 2nd fingers, between your 2nd and 3rd fingers, and between your 3rd and 4th fingers.

E♭
is played with low 1st finger on the D string.

Cello

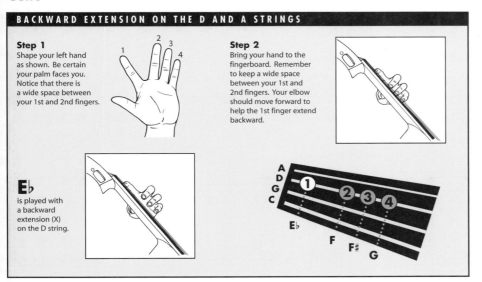

BACKWARD EXTENSION ON THE D AND A STRINGS

Step 1
Shape your left hand as shown. Be certain your palm faces you. Notice that there is a wide space between your 1st and 2nd fingers.

Step 2
Bring your hand to the fingerboard. Remember to keep a wide space between your 1st and 2nd fingers. Your elbow should move forward to help the 1st finger extend backward.

E♭
is played with a backward extension (X) on the D string.

Bass

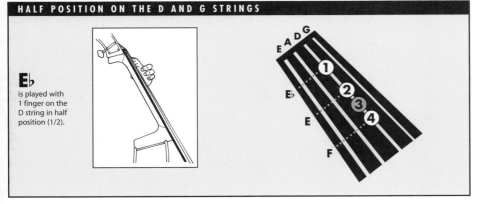

HALF POSITION ON THE D AND G STRINGS

E♭
is played with 1 finger on the D string in half position (1/2).

FLAT KEYS

Listening Skills   Play what your teacher plays. Listen carefully.

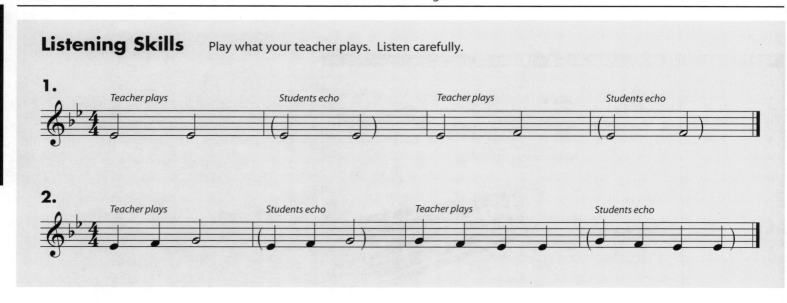

99. LET'S READ "E♭" (E-flat)

100. HOT CROSS BUNS

FLAT KEYS

Violin

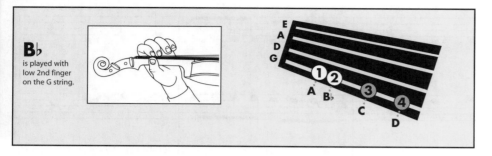

B♭ is played with low 2nd finger on the G string.

Viola

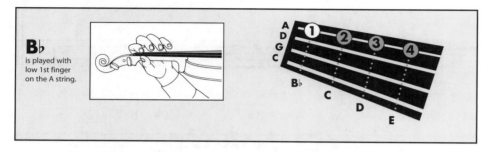

B♭ is played with low 1st finger on the A string.

Cello

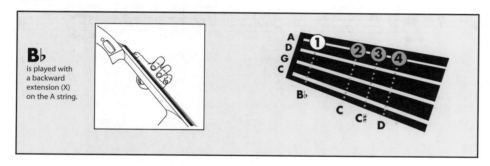

B♭ is played with a backward extension (X) on the A string.

Bass

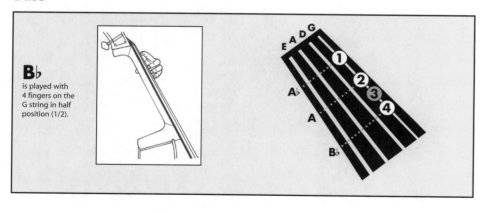

B♭ is played with 4 fingers on the G string in half position (1/2).

Teacher Prepare and reinforce student aural learning of B♭ by incorporating the following echo patterns for students.

Listening Skills   Play what your teacher plays. Listen carefully.

101. LET'S READ "B♭" (B-flat)

FLAT KEYS

102. VIKING WAY

Teacher   The objective of student book page 23 is to present the low B♭ scale (the B♭ scale beginning on the G string for violins, violas, and cellos).

103. HIKING ALONG

Key Signature: B♭ MAJOR

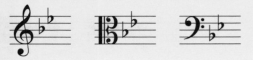

Play all B's as B♭ (B-flat) and all E's as E♭ (E-flat).

Teacher The B♭ Major key signature is introduced in 104, B♭ *Major Scale*. Review all previously learned major key signatures, e.g. D, G, C, and F. When learning the B♭ Major scale be certain that students play the B♭ and E♭ low enough. Have students practice the scale until their pitches are accurate and the scale is easily played.

104. B♭ MAJOR SCALE

FLAT KEYS

105. SLOVAKIAN FOLK SONG

106. CAVALIER COUNTRY

FLAT KEYS

Teacher   *Ayn Kaylokaynu* incorporates the concept of *A Tempo*. Explain the term and demonstrate how to apply it. Consider adding *A Tempo* to a review piece that students already know to reinforce their learning and to evaluate their understanding of this concept. Play different recordings of Jewish music. Have students analyze this style of music and describe how it is different from other styles of music they know.

QUIZ OBJECTIVES – AYN KAYLOKAYNU
- Hooked bowing
- Key of B♭ Major
- A Tempo
- Fermata
- Violin and Viola 4th finger on the G string

Review Exercises:
102. Viking Day
104. B♭ Major Scale
105. Slovakian Folk Song

107. ESSENTIAL ELEMENTS QUIZ – AYN KAYLOKAYNU

Traditional Jewish Song

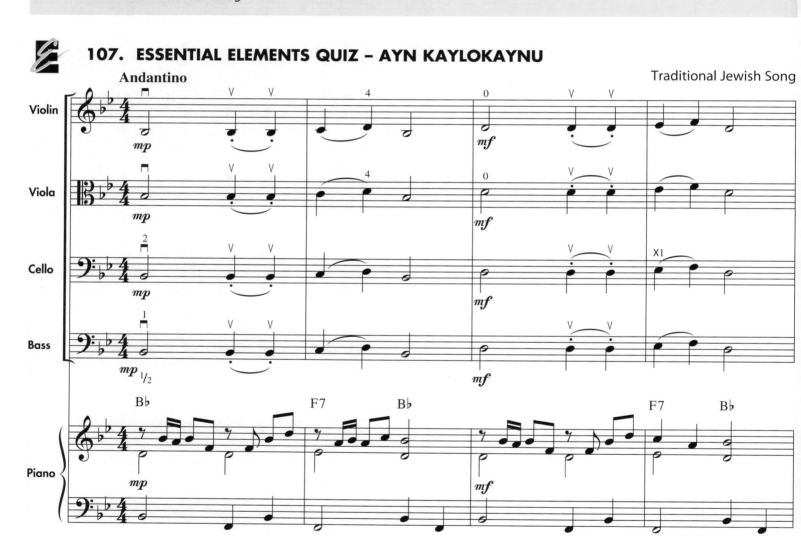

Violin/ Viola

On student book page 24 a new finger pattern is introduced for violin and viola: low fourth finger. Have students follow steps one and two, carefully shaping their hand as shown. For most students' hands, the tips of the third and fourth fingers should be touching for the low fourth finger to be in tune.

Students may practice by playing a pitch which uses their third finger, matching with an open string, and then placing their fourth finger next to it. Students may also prepare the shape of their hand by sliding their fourth finger back and forth, while keeping their other fingers in place on the string.

Violin

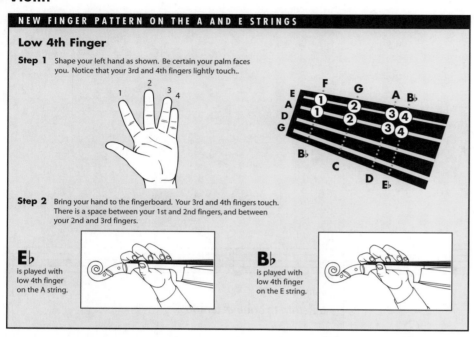

Viola

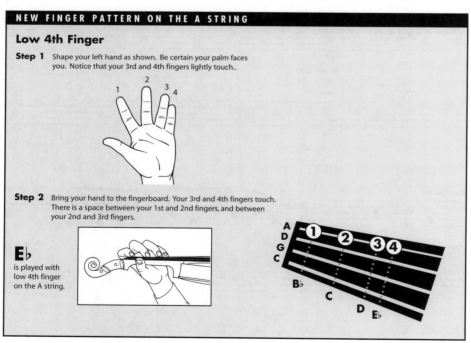

FLAT KEYS

Teacher While violins and violas are learning their new finger pattern, there is a special writing exercise in the cello and bass student books. The following answer key will assist you in checking their work quickly:

1. D	6. P	11. H	16. K
2. I	7. A	12. B	17. J
3. C	8. L	13. Q	18. R
4. N	9. G	14. O	
5. F	10. M	15. E	

Cello/Bass

Special Cello/Double Bass Exercise

While the violins and violas are learning new notes, match the following words with the correct definitions.
Write the correct letter of the definition in the blank next to the words.

1. _____ Staccato
2. _____ Allegro
3. _____ Slur
4. _____ Intonation
5. _____ Mezzo Forte
6. _____ Interval
7. _____ Crescendo
8. _____ Moderato
9. _____ Ritardando
10. _____ Allegretto
11. _____ Legato
12. _____ Fermata
13. _____ Decrescendo
14. _____ Lento
15. _____ Andante
16. _____ Tie
17. _____ Mezzo Piano
18. _____ Forte

A. Gradually increase volume
B. Hold the note (or rest) longer
C. Curved line that connects two or more different pitches
D. Play with a stopped bow stroke
E. Slower walking tempo
F. Moderately loud
G. Gradually slow the tempo
H. Play in a smooth and connected style
I. Fast tempo
J. Moderately soft
K. Curved line that connects notes of the same pitch
L. Medium tempo
M. Lively tempo, faster than Andante, but slower then Allegro
N. How well each note is played in tune
O. A very slow tempo
P. The distance between two notes
Q. Gradually decrease volume
R. Loud

FLAT KEYS

Teacher   Be sure students can accurately play the following echo sequences. They need to train their ear to be able to independently tune the pitch produced by their fourth finger.

Listening Skills   Play what your teacher plays. Listen carefully.

108. LET'S READ "E♭" (E-flat)

109. TECHNIQUE TRAX

FLAT KEYS

Teacher *Listening Skills* are included every time a new note is introduced. Research suggests that students with well-developed listening skills have better left/right hand coordination, intonation, and memorization skills.

Violin

B♭

Low 4th Finger

Violin Have violin students pull their bow faster on the E string to produce a desirable tone. Remember that notes on the E string require a faster bow speed compared to the other strings on the violin.

110. LET'S READ "B♭" (B-flat)

111. TECHNIQUE BUILDER

Teacher The objective of student book page 25 is to present and reinforce the upper octave B♭ Major scale on the violin. Opportunities for arranging music are also included.

Violin Be careful that students move their right elbow closer to their body when they prepare to cross from the A string to the E string. Have violins practice two octaves of the B♭ Major scale: the lower octave (exercise 104) and the upper octave (exercise 112).

112. B♭ MAJOR SCALE

FLAT KEYS

113. THE MOUNTAIN DEER CHASE

North American Folk Song

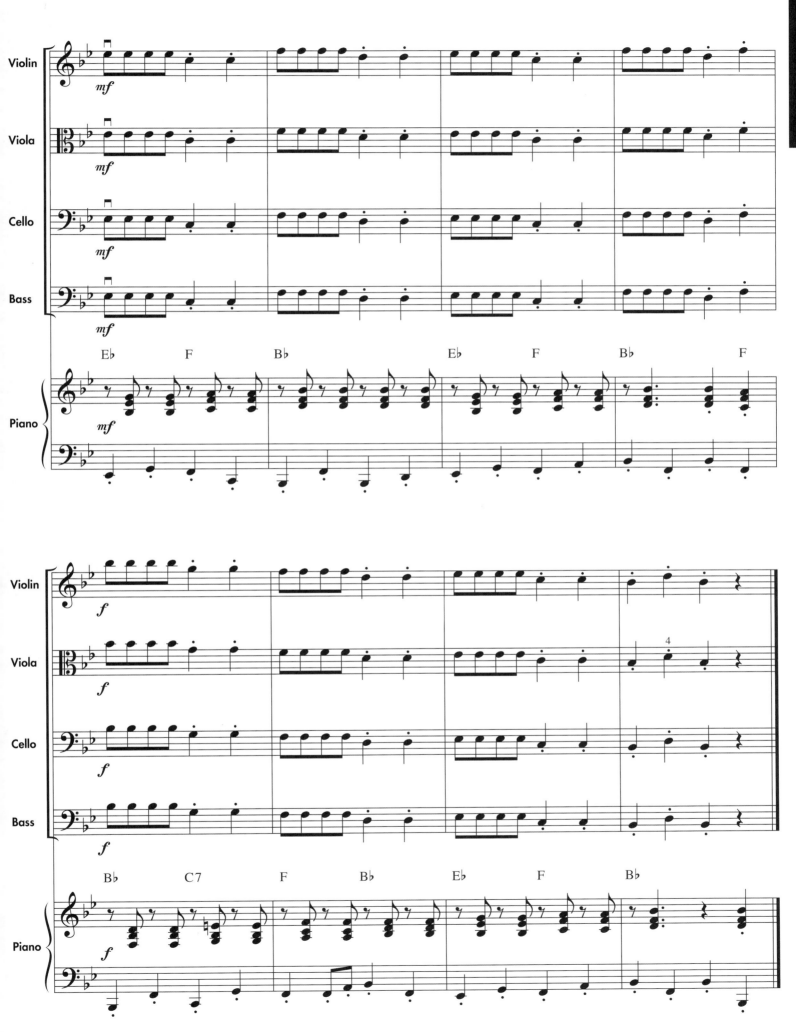

FLAT KEYS

Teacher   Introduce the concept of arranging music to students once they have learned to play *114. Essential Creativity – Rakes of Mallow*. Explain and demonstrate how changing the rhythms, phrases, and/or styles of the original can create simple arrangements. Give students the opportunity to perform their arrangements for their classmates. This also allows you the opportunity to assess their rhythmic and stylistic development.

114. ESSENTIAL CREATIVITY – RAKES OF MALLOW

Irish Folk Song

All Instruments

Music can be created and arranged by changing rhythms and notes to an existing example. Create your own arrangement of *Rakes of Mallow* by changing the rhythms and melodic phrases. Perform your arrangement for others.

Example 1: Changing rhythms   *Example 2: Changing melodic phrases*

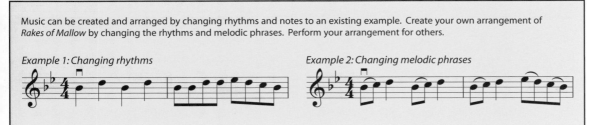

THEORY

6/8 RHYTHMS

$\frac{6}{8}$ Time Signature

$\frac{6}{8}$ $\frac{6}{8}$ $\frac{6}{8}$ = **6 beats** per measure

                                    = **Eighth** note gets one beat

6/8 time is usually played with a slight emphasis on the **1st** and **4th** beats of each measure. This divides the measure into 2 groups of 3 beats each.

♪ = 1 beat   ♩ = 2 beats

♩. = 3 beats   ♩♪ = 6 beats

Teacher   The objective of student book page 26 is to introduce $\frac{6}{8}$ meter. It is first introduced at a slow tempo, with six beats to a measure. Students are encouraged to place a small accent on beats 1 and 4. A slight lean on their bow stick with their index finger on those beats, or pulling their bow faster on them, will accomplish this. Be sure students count and tap while playing. Practice shadow bowing *115. Rhythm Rap,* in the air and then on an open string. Be sure students count and tap while playing. Demonstrate for students how their bow speed must slow down for dotted quarter notes and dotted half notes as compared to the eighth note.

115. RHYTHM RAP   *Shadow bow and count before playing.*

116. LAZY DAY

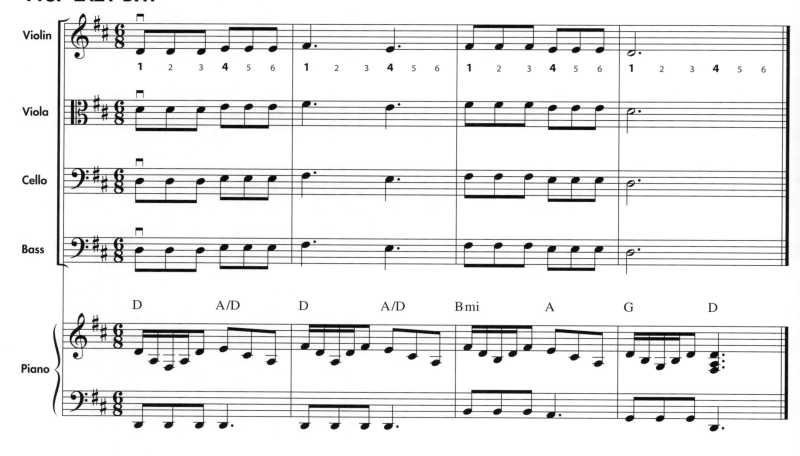

117. HOOKED ON 6/8

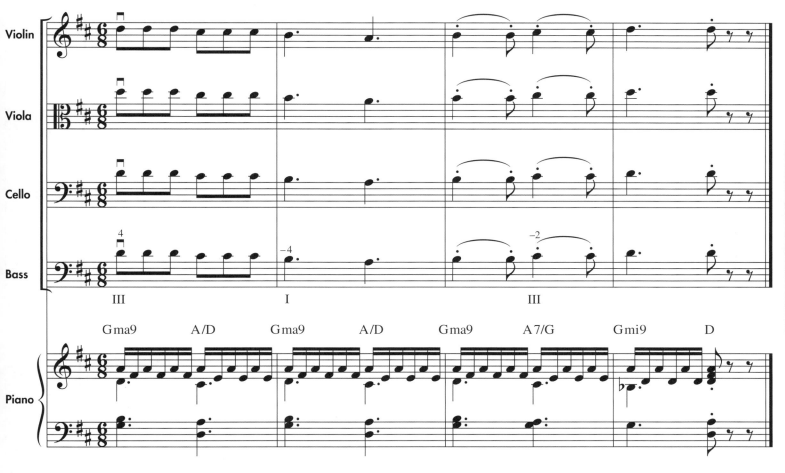

Musical Form

A round is a **musical form** where performers play or sing the same melody, entering at different times. This is called counterpoint, a type of harmony. Try memorizing this round and performing it with a friend.

Teacher Read and discuss the definition of a *round*. Explain that a *round* is an example of a *musical form*. Point out to students that they have already been playing simple rounds earlier, e.g. *10. G Major Scale Round* (student book page 4). Play a round for the class and have the students identify the characteristics aurally.

118. Row, Row, Row Your Boat is included to help students learn to feel $\frac{6}{8}$ at a slow tempo within a musical context. The large circled numbers above the staff show students when new entrances begin when performing this selection as a round. The words to the song *Row, Row, Row Your Boat* are provided in the back of the *Teacher's Manual*, on page 289, for use with your students. Ask your class to sing it as a round.

118. ROW, ROW, ROW YOUR BOAT – Round

American Folk Round

(Repeat as needed for round)

119. SLURRING IN 6/8 TIME

Teacher Students should begin to play *120. Jolly Good Fellow,* in the lower half of the bow, even though the first stroke is up bow. This allows students enough bow to play the correct bowing in measure one. Explain and demonstrate to students that an up bow stroke or a down bow stroke may start at any place in the bow. Students often believe that an up bow may only start in the upper half of the bow and a down bow only in the lower half. However, the placement of the stroke actually depends on the length of the upbeat note and the notes that follow.

The words are provided in the back of the *Teacher's Manual,* on page 289, for your use. Have your students sing it as a solo and in groups.

120. JOLLY GOOD FELLOW

Teacher The objective of student book page 27 is to introduce faster tempo $\frac{6}{8}$ meter.

$\frac{6}{8}$ Time Signature

When music in $\frac{6}{8}$ time is played fast, it is easier to stress beats one and four, and "feel" the pulse in two large beats.

Counted in 6 = **1** 2 3 **4** 5 6
Counted in 2 = **1** & a **2** & a

THEORY

Teacher In *121. Rhythm Rap,* $\frac{6}{8}$ meter is now introduced at a faster tempo, where it is felt and played with two beats to a measure. Be sure students count and tap while shadow bowing exercise 121. Students should completely stop their bows between the hooked notes in measure three.

6 / 8 RHYTHMS

121. RHYTHM RAP *Shadow bow and count before playing.*

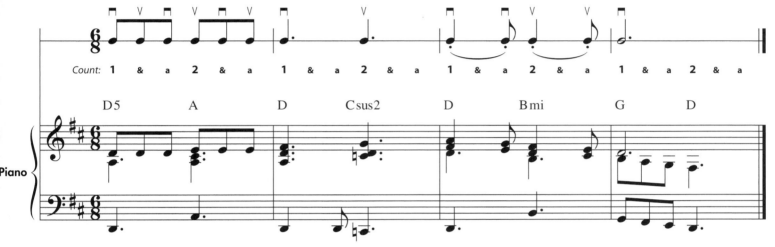

122. RISE AND FALL

6/8 RHYTHMS

Teacher   Students should write in a $\frac{6}{8}$ time signature before playing *Beach Walk*.

123. BEACH WALK

▼ *Write in the correct time signature before you begin.*

HISTORY

Austrian composer **Wolfgang Amadeus Mozart** was a child prodigy who lived during the American Revolution. At five, he was composing music, and by his early teens he had mastered the violin. Mozart wrote more than 600 compositions during his short life, including oratorios, symphonies, concertos, and operas. Imagine and describe the career of a composer.

Teacher   Discuss the life and musical contribution of Mozart. Play examples of his recorded works. Explain how a composer during his lifetime primarily made money composing through commissions. Composers were often at the whim of the musical styles and tastes of those with money who commissioned works. Describe how some composers, especially Mozart, found this constraining and aggravating.

124. MAY TIME

W. A. Mozart (1756–1791)

6/8 RHYTHMS

MINOR KEYS

Teacher The objective of student book pages 28 and 29 is to present minor scales. D and G minor (natural) scales are presented, and related key signatures.

THEORY

Minor Scales

A minor scale is a series of eight notes which follow a definite pattern of whole steps and half steps. There are three forms of the minor scale; natural minor, harmonic minor, and melodic minor. The D minor (natural) scale uses the same pitches as the F major scale.

Teacher Have students sustain each pitch of the D minor (natural) scale to prepare them for exercise 125, checking their understanding of the sequence of half steps and whole steps while listening carefully for intonation. Check to see if cellos are extending backward properly for B♭. Transpose the scale pattern and have students learn to play the G minor (natural) scale as well (No. 129). Ask students to describe how a minor scale sounds different from a major scale.

125. D MINOR (Natural) SCALE

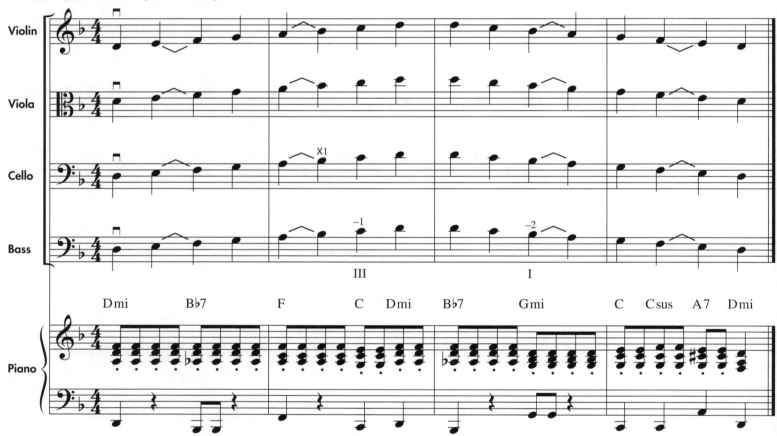

HISTORY Austrian composer **Gustav Mahler** was also a successful conductor. He believed in unifying the arts and often combined music, poetry, and philosophy in his compositions. Exercise 126 *Mahler's Theme* first appears in his *Symphony No. 1*, played as a solo by the double bass. During Mahler's lifetime Vincent van Gogh created his most famous paintings, and Mark Twain wrote *Tom Sawyer*.

Teacher Play recordings of Mahler's music and discuss his life and music, as well as art created during the Romantic period. Especially feature his *Symphony No. 1*. Students can hear the opening bass solo from the last movement of that work, featured in *126. Mahler's Theme*. Play recordings of two different bass soloists playing this solo and ask students to analyze and describe the differences in the performances. Also, note that this line can be played in class as a round. Entrances are marked with circled numbers. Help students compare major and minor tonalities by giving them the opportunity to play *Mahler's Theme* in D Major. Ask students to describe the difference between major and minor tonalities.

126. MAHLER'S THEME – Round

Gustav Mahler (1860–1911)

(Repeat as needed for round)

MINOR KEYS

Teacher   *Shalom Chaverim* and *The Snake Charmer* are unison melodies in D minor (natural) to reinforce student learning of the key. Note that *Shalom Chaverim* can be played as a round.

127. SHALOM CHAVERIM – Round

Hebrew Folk Song

Student books have 1 measure in 2nd ending.

128. THE SNAKE CHARMER

MINOR KEYS

Key Signature: G MINOR

The G minor (natural) scale uses the same pitches as the B♭ major scale.

Teacher Point out to students that the G minor (natural) scale is played with the same fingerings and half and whole step patterns as the D minor (natural) scale, beginning on the G string rather than the D string for violin, viola, and cello.

129. G MINOR (Natural) SCALE

HISTORY

With the establishment of Israel as an independent political state in 1948, *Hatikvah* became the Israeli National Anthem. The same year Mohandas Gandhi was assassinated in India. Israeli violinists Itzhak Perlman and Pinchas Zukerman are concert artists known throughout the world.

Teacher When discussing Israel and its history, inform students of the great string and orchestra tradition in Israel. Many of the greatest orchestral and solo string performers have come from Israel. Play sample recordings of music with Israeli violinists Itzhak Perlman and Pinchas Zukerman to inspire yourself and your students. Ask students to analyze the quality of the performances on the recordings they hear, discussing the artists tone production, intonation, and musical phrasing. Inform your students that these recordings are made by professional musicians. Discuss the various aspects of a career as a concert artist.

Hatikvah, composed by Naftali Herz Imber (1856–1909), is the national anthem of Israel. Hatikvah means "The Hope." Hatikva expresses the hope of the Jewish people, that they would someday return to the land of their forefathers as prophesied in the Old Testament.

130. HATIKVAH

Israeli National Anthem

Student books have repeats, not 1st and 2nd endings.

MINOR KEYS

Student books have repeats, not 1st and 2nd endings.

Violin Violin students are now ready to learn to play the upper octave of the G minor (natural) scale. Point out that the half and whole step patterns are the same as those in the lower octave G minor (natural scale), exercise 129. Have violin students combine the lower and upper octaves of the scales to produce a two-octave G minor (natural) scale.

131. G MINOR (Natural) SCALE

MINOR KEYS

Teacher   *The Hanukkah Song* is one of many Israeli folk songs. The Hebrew words appear in the Teacher's Manual on page 289. Discuss the celebration of Hanukkah within the Jewish culture.

QUIZ OBJECTIVES – THE HANUKKAH SONG

- G minor (natural) key
- E♭
- B♭
- Sudden dynamic changes

Review Exercises:

129. *G Minor (Natural) Scale (lower octave)*

130. *Hatikvah*

131. *G Minor (Natural) Scale (violin upper octave)*

132. ESSENTIAL ELEMENTS QUIZ – THE HANUKKAH SONG

Israeli Folk Song

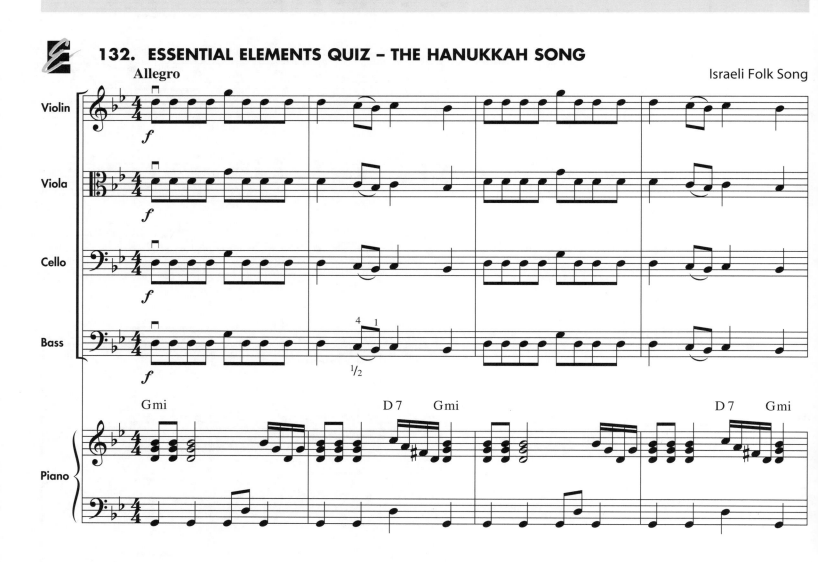

Mixed Meter

Occasionally the meter (time signature) changes in music. Watch for meter changes and count carefully.

Teacher The primary objective of student book page 30 is to introduce meter changes within a piece. Explain and demonstrate the application of meter changes in *133. Rhythm Rap*. Then apply this in a musical context to *French Folk Song*, and *Kum Ba Yah*. Point out to students that in all of these examples the quarter note pulse remains the same regardless of the number of pulses per measure. Be sure students count and tap while playing.

The term *Cantabile* also is introduced on student book page 30.

MIXED METER

133. RHYTHM RAP *Shadow bow and count before playing.*

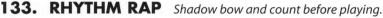
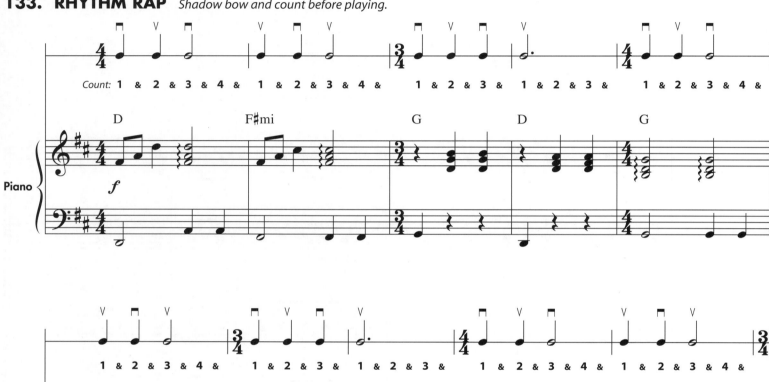

MIXED METER

134. FRENCH FOLK SONG

MIXED METER

MIXED METER

Teacher   Explain and demonstrate the meaning of the term *cantabile* in *135. Kum Ba Yah.* Contrast for students the sound of staccato and cantabile to help them understand the meaning of the term.

THEORY				
Cantabile	In a singing style.		**e**	The Italian word for "and."

Teacher   The words to *Kum Ba Yah,* are provided on page 288 for your use. Have students volunteer to sing it by themselves or with others in class. Play different recordings of spirituals or gospel music. Have students analyze this style of music and describe how it is different from other styles of music.

135. KUM BA YAH

African Spiritual

MIXED METER

MIXED METER

THEORY

Triplets

A **triplet** is a group of three notes. In $\frac{2}{4}$, $\frac{3}{4}$, or $\frac{4}{4}$ time, an eighth note triplet is spread evenly across one beat.

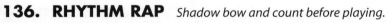

Teacher The objective of student book page 36 is to introduce triplets. Define triplets as explained in the student book and demonstrate how they are counted and played. Be sure students count and tap accurately while shadow bowing *136. Rhythm Rap.*

RHYTHMS

136. RHYTHM RAP *Shadow bow and count before playing.*

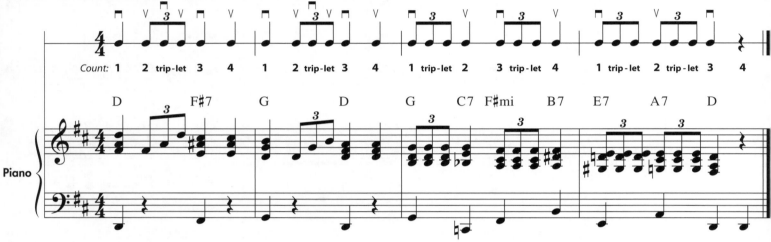

Teacher Transpose *D Major Scale With Triplets,* to any of the major or minor scales students have previously learned.

137. D MAJOR SCALE WITH TRIPLETS

138. ON THE MOVE

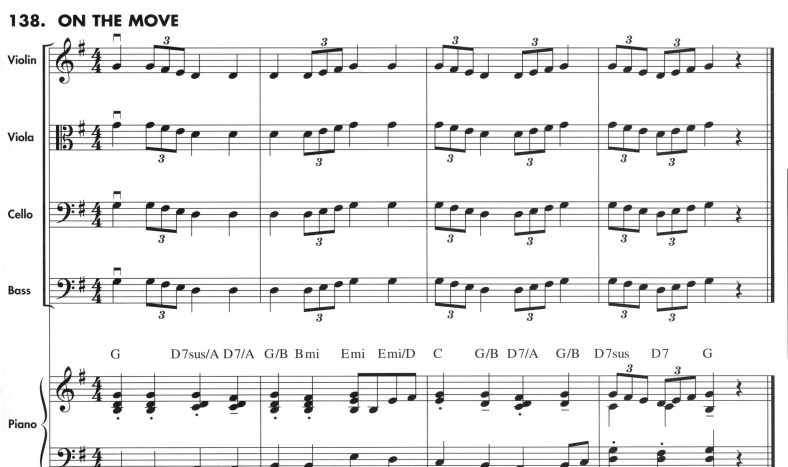

RHYTHMS

139. SLURRING TRIPLETS

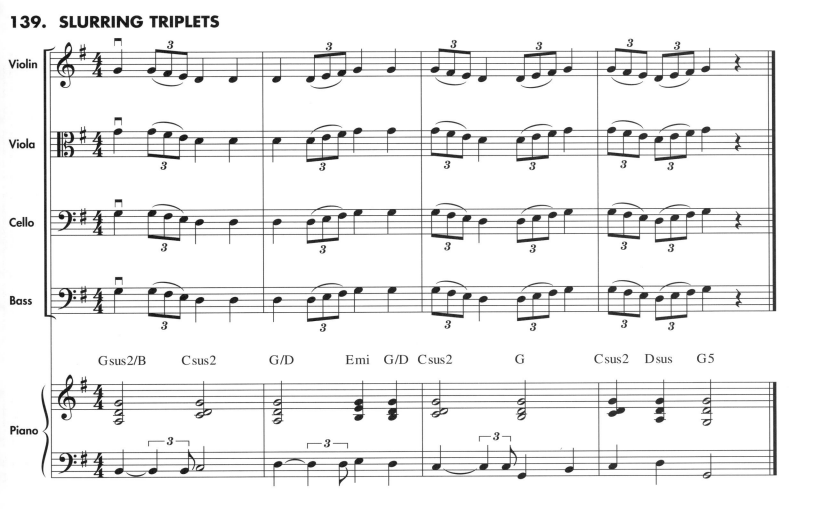

140. TRIPLET ETUDE

141. LITTLE RIVER

Teacher   When preparing to teach *Field Song,* compare examples of southern American folksongs such as *Bile 'em Cabbages Down* with northern American folksongs, like *Yankee Doodle Dandy.* Discuss how native folk songs unite people and express their unique life and culture.

142. FIELD SONG

Southern American Folk Song

THEORY

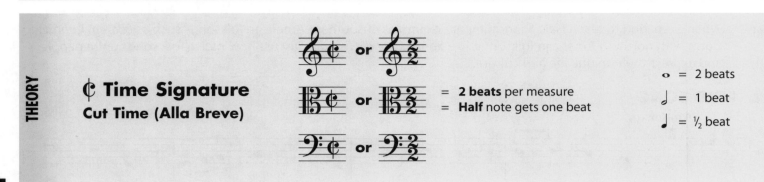

¢ **Time Signature**
Cut Time (Alla Breve)

= **2 beats** per measure
= **Half** note gets one beat

𝅝 = 2 beats
𝅗𝅥 = 1 beat
♩ = ½ beat

RHYTHMS

Teacher The objective of student book pages 32 and 33 is to introduce the cut time signature. Point out to students that the cut time signature ¢ and the $\frac{2}{2}$ time signature are the same: there are two major pulses in each measure and each pulse gets one count. Compare this time signature with those with a quarter note as the main pulse, e.g $\frac{2}{4}$, $\frac{3}{4}$, and $\frac{4}{4}$.

Practice counting, tapping, clapping, and shadow bowing *143. Rhythm Rap*, in cut time. Then, practice and count it in $\frac{4}{4}$ time so students feel and understand the difference between $\frac{4}{4}$ time and cut time. Use the same procedure for teaching exercise 144.

143. RHYTHM RAP *Shadow bow and count before playing.*

144. A CUT ABOVE

RHYTHMS

145. CUT TIME MARCH

146. RHYTHM RAP   *Shadow bow and count before playing.*

147. SYNCOPATION MARCH

RHYTHMS

Teacher   The words to the song *When the Saints Go Marchin' In* are provided in the back of the *Teacher's Manual,* page 288. Feel free to make copies of the words for your students to sing. Students can sing the melody while you accompany them on the piano or while listening to the *Play-Along Trax* accompaniment.

148. WHEN THE SAINTS GO MARCHIN' IN

James M. Black

Are you counting in cut time?

Teacher   The objective of student book page 33 is to introduce cut time in rhythms involving eighth notes. Explain and demonstrate for students how eighth notes are counted differently in cut time compared to $\frac{2}{4}$, $\frac{3}{4}$, and $\frac{4}{4}$ time.

149. RHYTHM RAP   *Shadow bow and count before playing.*

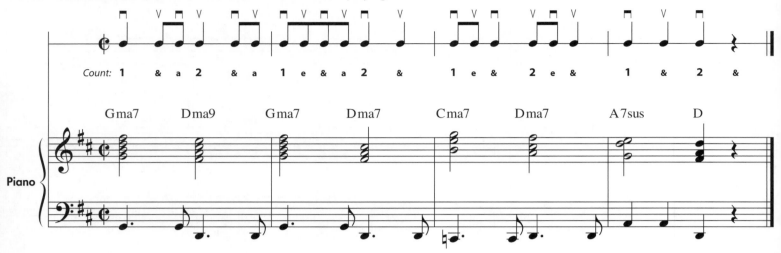

150. DOWN HOME

151. MOVING ALONG

RHYTHMS

152. RHYTHM RAP *Shadow bow and count before playing.*

153. UP TOWN

154. FLYING BOWS

RHYTHMS

HISTORY

Cantatas are pieces much like short operas that were written during the **Baroque Period** (1600–1750). They involve vocal soloists and choirs that are accompanied by small orchestras. **Johann Sebastian Bach** wrote nearly 300 of them between 1704 and 1745. While Bach was composing his cantatas, the famous philosopher Voltaire was writing his books and Thomas Jefferson, the great United States president, was born.

Teacher   A melody from Bach's *Peasant Cantata* is presented in *155. March From Peasant's Cantata*. Describe what cantatas are, and also discuss the works of Voltaire. Point out other historical events that were occurring in America at the same time, such as the birth of Thomas Jefferson. Play recordings of other Bach cantatas and have students describe the style of the music and evaluate the quality of the performances.

155. MARCH FROM PEASANT'S CANTATA

J. S. Bach (1685–1750)

RHYTHMS

Teacher A PERFORMANCE SPOTLIGHT appears on student book pages 34–37. The objective of these pages is to summarize some of the principal playing skills the students have learned in this book. These pieces may be used in a special concert performance, or at any time you choose. Different styles of music are included to provide a varied musical experience for both the audience and performers. You may, of course, play these arrangements at any time once the necessary skills have been mastered. The required playing skills are provided for each arrangement.

Encourage students to evaluate their performances. Self-assessment is critical to the overall development of playing skills. Suggest to students that they use criteria such as tone production, intonation, rhythm, tempo, dynamics, and musical style to evaluate their performance.

Remind students what proper concert etiquette is for both performers and audience members. Students also should be reminded that they must practice their music until it is mastered before performing. Review with them what is appropriate concert dress. Remind them that they must arrive early before the concert begins so that they have adequate time to tune and warm up.

PERFORMANCE SPOTLIGHT

Performing music for others is fun and rewarding. Either small or large ensembles can perform the following arrangements. Always observe proper concert etiquette by being well prepared, dressing appropriately, being on time, and remembering all equipment. Show respect when others are playing by listening attentively and applauding at the appropriate time.

Teacher Remember that in A-B part arrangements the A parts are almost the same for all instruments. The B parts are different for each instrument. To achieve the fullest orchestral sound, have half of the violins play the A part and half play the B part. The other instruments should play their B part. Of course, any instrument section may be featured on the melody (part A), while the other instrument sections play their B parts.

156. Sagebrush Overture, is an orchestra arrangement of two famous melodies from Texas: *The Streets of Laredo* and *The Yellow Rose of Texas.* Enjoy!

Playing skills necessary for 156:

- $\frac{3}{4}$ time
- $\frac{2}{4}$ time
- Meter Change
- Dotted Quarter Notes
- Détaché Bowing
- Staccato Bowing
- Hooked Bowing
- Syncopation
- Cello Extensions
- Violin/Viola Extended Third Fingers

PERFORMANCE SPOTLIGHT

156. SAGEBRUSH OVERTURE – Orchestra Arrangement

A = Melody. **B** = Harmony. For orchestra, half the violins play each part.

Arr. John Higgins

PERFORMANCE SPOTLIGHT

PERFORMANCE SPOTLIGHT

✔ What were the strong points of your performance?

Teacher   Explain to students the dynamic marking *mp* – *f* at the beginning of *Pomp And Circumstance – Orchestra Arrangement*. Students need to understand that they should play *mp* through the first ending and *f* on the repeat. This excellent arrangement can be played by string orchestra for school graduations.

Playing skills necessary for 157:
- Détaché Bowing
- Staccato Bowing
- Hooked Bowing
- Syncopation
- First/Second Endings
- C Major, F# accidental

Play recordings of other music by Edward Elgar and have students analyze his music and evaluate the quality of the performances they hear. The theme of his *Enigma Variations* is for strings only and is an especially good example for young string players to hear how expressive string instruments can sound.

157. POMP AND CIRCUMSTANCE – Orchestra Arrangement

Edward Elgar (1857–1933)
Arr. John Higgins

Teacher   The words to *America The Beautiful,* are provided in the *Teacher's Manual* on page 288 for your use. Have students volunteer to sing *America The Beautiful* as a solo or with other members of the class.

Playing skills necessary for 158:
- Détaché Bowing
- Staccato Bowing
- Hooked Bowing
- Legato Bowing
- Two-Note Slurs
- Crescendo/Decrescendo
- Ritard.
- G Major, C♯ accidental

158. AMERICA THE BEAUTIFUL – Orchestra Arrangement

Samuel Augustus Ward (1847–1903)
Arr. John Higgins

Teacher Point out to students the *D.C. al Fine* in *La Bamba – Duet*. Remind them to play until *D.C. al Fine*, and then go back to the beginning and play to the *Fine*.

Playing skills necessary for 159:

- Détaché Bowing
- Accents
- Hooked Bowing
- Eighth Notes
- D.C. al Fine
- G Major

159. LA BAMBA – Duet

Mexican Folk Song
Arr. Michael Allen

PERFORMANCE SPOTLIGHT

HISTORY

Gustav Holst was a famous British orchestra composer who frequently set words to music, including poems by the American poet, Walt Whitman. Holst's *St. Paul's Suite* for string orchestra was written for the St. Paul's Girls School Orchestra and published in 1913. His best known work is *The Planets,* first performed in 1918, the same year as the end of World War I.

Teacher   Review the *History* section on student book page 36 regarding the life and musical contributions of the composer Gustav Holst. Play a recording and show the score of his great string orchestra masterpiece, *St. Paul's Suite.* His full-orchestra work, *The Planets,* is an audience favorite throughout Europe and America. There are many professional recordings of the work available to play for your students' enjoyment.

Playing skills necessary for 160:
- Détaché Bowing
- Two-Note Slurs
- Dotted Quarter-Eighth Note Rhythm
- F Major
- Ritard
- Decrescendo

160. IN THE BLEAK MIDWINTER – Orchestra Arrangement

Gustav Holst (1874–1934)
Arr. John Higgins

PERFORMANCE SPOTLIGHT

PERFORMANCE SPOTLIGHT

Teacher   An orchestra arrangement of the melody *Swallowtail Jig* appears on student book page 37. Show students how the melody and accompaniment are based on arpeggios and tetrachords.

Playing skills necessary for 161:
- Hooked Bowing
- $\frac{6}{8}$ meter
- Two-Note Slurs
- Three-Note Slurs
- Repeat
- First and Second Endings

161. SWALLOWTAIL JIG – Orchestra Arrangement

Irish Jig
Arr. John Higgins

PERFORMANCE SPOTLIGHT

PERFORMANCE SPOTLIGHT

Sight-reading

Sight-reading means playing a musical piece for the first time. The key to sight-reading success is to know what to look for *before* you play. Use the word **S-T-A-R-S** to remind yourself what to look for, and eventually your orchestra will become sight-reading STARS!

S — **Sharps or flats** in the key signature

T — **Time signature** and **tempo markings**

A — **Accidentals** not found in the key signature

R — **Rhythms**, silently counting the more difficult notes and rests

S — **Signs**, including dynamics, articulations, repeats and endings

Teacher The objective of student book page 38 is to provide your students the opportunity to develop the important skill of sight-reading. Review the STARS acronym with your students and encourage them to memorize it. The following is a shorter version of STARS to help students with their memorization:

S	Sharps or flats in the key signature
T	Time signature and tempos
A	Accidentals
R	Rhythm
S	Signs

Discuss each element of sight-reading as it pertains to the exercises on student book page 38. Once students have mastered sight-reading these lines give them solo or orchestra music that they have never seen before. Ask them to apply the STARS acronym to this music and then sight-read it.

162. SIGHT-READING CHALLENGE #1

163. SIGHT-READING CHALLENGE #2

164. SIGHT-READING CHALLENGE #3

165. SIGHT-READING CHALLENGE #4

PREPARING FOR HIGHER POSITIONS

Natural Harmonic

THEORY

Natural harmonics are tones created by a vibrating string divided into equal sections. To play an octave higher than an open string, lightly touch the string exactly half way between the bridge and the nut. In the following examples, harmonics are indicated by a "○" above a note, plus a fingering number. ⁴○ indicates a harmonic played with the fourth finger.

Teacher The objective of student book page 39 is to prepare students for higher positions and shifting. These skills are thoroughly and sequentially presented in *Essential Technique for Strings* and *Advanced Technique for Strings*.

Review the definition of harmonics. Show students how lightly they must touch the string to produce harmonics. Also, instruct students to pull their bow lighter and faster than they normally would for the best sound. Show students that the harmonics that appear in exercises 166–169 are located on the string about half way between the bridge and nut.

166.

HARMONICS/SHIFTING

167.

168.

△ *New Note: A*

△ *New Note: A*

HARMONICS/SHIFTING

169.

HARMONICS/SHIFTING

Shifting

Sliding your left hand smoothly and lightly to a new location on the fingerboard, indicated by a dash (–). Be sure your thumb moves with your hand.

Teacher The concept of shifting to harmonics is introduced in exercises 170–173. Read the definition of shifting to the students and demonstrate it for them. Point out that their fingers should slide lightly on top of the strings when shifting. Also show them that their thumb should travel with their hand during a shift. Point out to students that the dash in front of a fingering indicates a shift.

170.

171.

172.

173.

Violin
Viola

The objective of student book pages 40 and 41 is to summarize for students the four basic left-hand finger patterns for violin and viola. Organizing finger spacing into patterns helps students understand quickly and efficiently how to play in different keys.

Hand drawings are used to show students the correct finger spacing for each finger pattern. These different finger patterns are referred to as the open hand, 1–2, 2–3, and 3–4 finger patterns.

Each exercise on student book page 40 incorporates a finger pattern and the pitches it would sound on each of the four strings.

Practice each exercise until students understand and have mastered the finger pattern on all strings. You may also have students mark the half steps to help them understand the finger spacing in each pattern.

Please note that the finger patterns do not apply to lower strings, only violin and viola. The cellos and basses do have new shifts occasionally, but they follow a logical sequence for ease of understanding and performance.

Violin/Viola

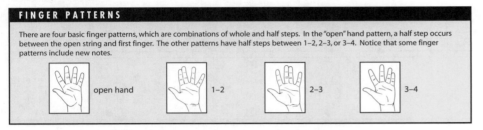

FINGER PATTERNS

There are four basic finger patterns, which are combinations of whole and half steps. In the "open" hand pattern, a half step occurs between the open string and first finger. The other patterns have half steps between 1–2, 2–3, or 3–4. Notice that some finger patterns include new notes.

open hand   1–2   2–3   3–4

Cello/Bass

FINGER PATTERNS (violin and viola)

While the violins and violas are practicing various finger patterns, you will be playing some new notes in new positions. All new positions are indicated with a ★ and shifts with a −. Remember to slide your hand smoothly and lightly to the new location. Always keep your thumb behind your second finger.

FINGER PATTERNS (By Pattern)

174. 3–4 PATTERN (violin, viola)

Side tab: **FINGER PATTERNS**

FINGER PATTERNS

175. 2–3 PATTERN (violin, viola)

G String

C String

176. 1–2 PATTERN (violin, viola)

FINGER PATTERNS

177. OPEN PATTERN (violin, viola)

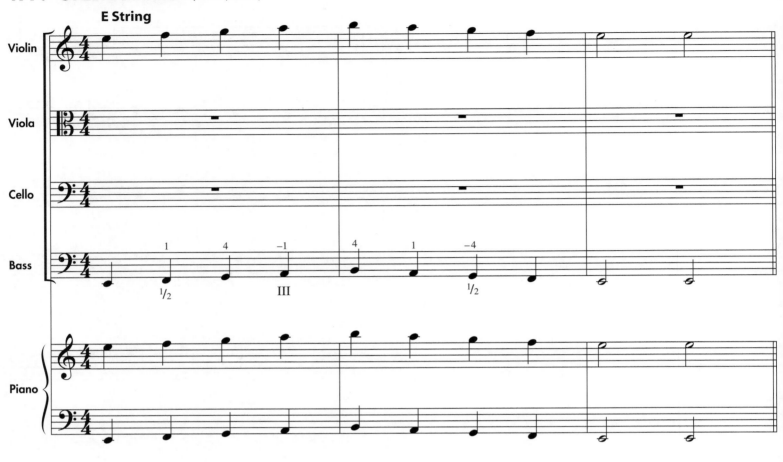

G String

C String

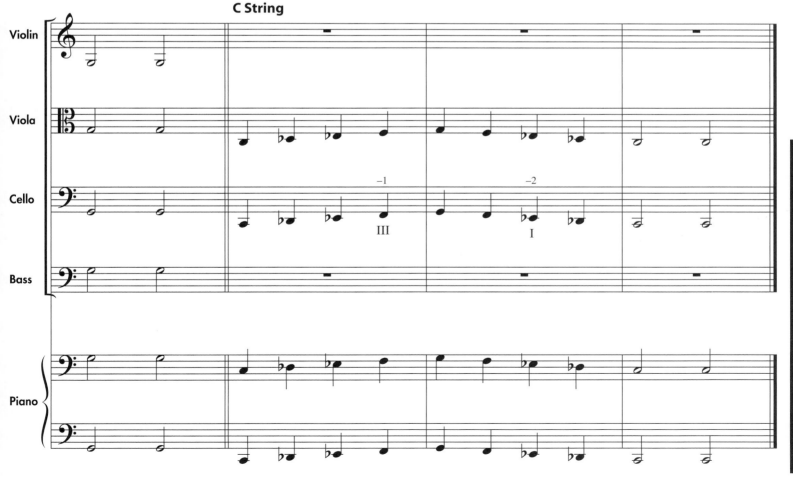

FINGER PATTERNS

FINGER PATTERNS (By String)

Violin/Viola   Finger patterns on student book page 41 are grouped by string, e.g. all finger patterns and their pitches are shown as a group on each string per exercise.

As students master and understand the finger patterns have them use different bowings and rhythms to play the exercises. Also, consider having students play the exercises from memory as part of their orchestra warm-up.

178. E STRING (violin, bass)

Open Pattern

179. A STRING

Open Pattern

180. D STRING

Open Pattern

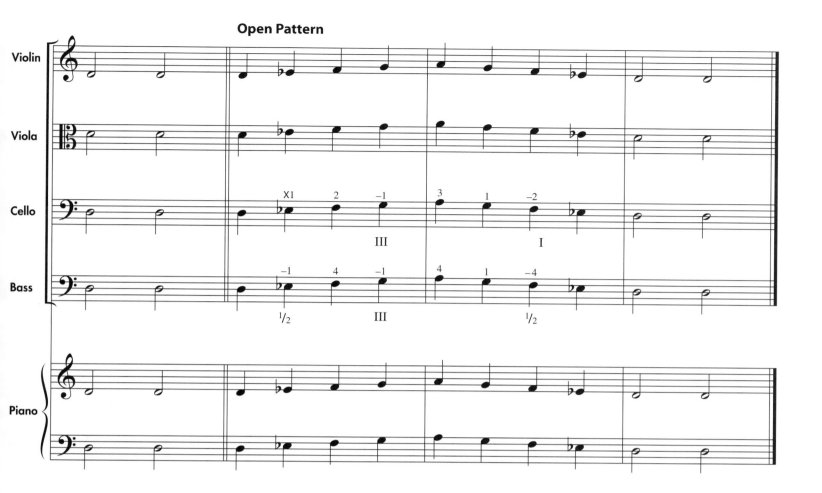

181. G STRING

Open Pattern

182. C STRING *(viola, cello)*

**Violin/
Viola**
The objective of student book pages 42 and 43 is to present violin and viola finger patterns organized by key. A hand drawing showing the correct finger spacing appears over each string in a particular key. Once students learn the finger patterns in each key they may transfer that understanding to any piece they are learning.

Evaluate students' knowledge of finger patterns by giving them new music and asking them to determine the finger patterns necessary to play it. You may also announce for students a key and a string and ask them to hold their left hand up in the air and show you the proper finger spacing for that key and string.

FINGER PATTERNS (By Key)

183. C MAJOR

184. G MAJOR

185. D MAJOR

186. A MAJOR

187. F MAJOR

188. B♭ MAJOR

SCALES AND ARPEGGIOS

 Identify two important elements of performing scales and arpeggios accurately.
As you play each line, check to make sure you are able to do these things.

Teacher The objective of student book pages 44 and 45 is to present all scales that appear in this book. The appropriate octave range for each instrument is indicated on the student pages. Assign different bowings, articulations, and dynamics to the scales and arpeggios as students practice. You also may want to group the scales together by finger patterns to help students review them efficiently. Students will be able to continue to master these scales and arpeggios in *Essential Technique for Strings*.

As students practice the scale and arpeggios, discuss with them elements of their playing to evaluate so that they may continue to learn to assess their performance, e.g. tone production, rhythm, intonation, articulation, and use of the correct finger patterns on the violin and viola. The EE check asks students to design their own criteria for evaluating their playing skills. Be certain that students are doing these things while playing each line.

189. C MAJOR

190. C MAJOR *(Lower Octave – viola and cello)*

191. G MAJOR

192. G MAJOR *(Upper Octave – violin)*

193. D MAJOR

194. D MAJOR *(Lower Octave – viola and cello)*

195. A MAJOR

196. A MAJOR *(Upper Octave – violin)*

197. F MAJOR

198. B♭ MAJOR

199. B♭ MAJOR *(Upper Octave – violin)*

200. D MINOR (Natural)

201. D MINOR (Natural)   *(Lower Octave – viola and cello)*

SCALES AND ARPEGGIOS

202. G MINOR (Natural)

203. G MINOR (Natural) *(Upper Octave – violin)*

CREATING MUSIC

Teacher The objective of student book page 46 is to give students the opportunity to create their own music, either by improvising or composing. For exercise 204 have students select pitches from those specified and write them in line A. Students may use any rhythms they want, but point out to them that there must be four pulses in each measure since the exercise is written in $\frac{4}{4}$ time. Have students add slurring or bow articulations, e.g. staccato, accents, two or four note slurs. Suggest that they also add dynamics.

Once the students have written their improvisation give them an opportunity to perform, while accompanied by the orchestra playing part B or the recorded track. Students may also practice their improvisations in class or at home with the recorded track.

THEORY

Improvisation   **Improvisation** is the art of freely creating your own music as you play.

204. *Using the following notes, improvise your own melody (Line A) to go with the accompaniment (Line B).*

IMPROVISATION/COMPOSITION

Composition

THEORY

Composition is the art of writing original music. A composer often begins by creating a melody made up of individual **phrases**, like short musical "sentences." Some melodies have phrases that seem to answer or respond to "question" phrases, as in Beethoven's *Ode To Joy*. Play this melody and listen to how phrase 2 answers phrase 1.

Teacher Study with students the question/answer phrases in *205. Ode to Joy*. In exercise *206. Phrase Builders*, and exercise *207. Q. And A.*, students are given the opportunity to complete phrases with musical answers. Point out the question phrase usually ends on something other than the tonic and that the best answers end on the tonic.

205. ODE TO JOY

Ludwig van Beethoven (1770–1827)

IMPROVISATION/COMPOSITION

206. PHRASE BUILDERS *Write 2 different phrases using the following rhythms.*

A

B

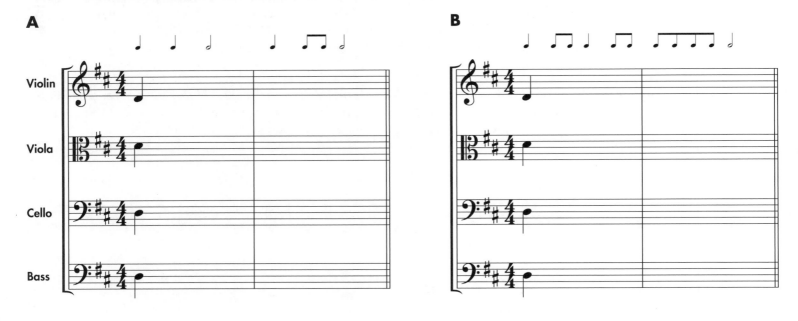

207. Q. AND A. *Write your own "answer" to the following melodies.*

IMPROVISATION/COMPOSITION

Teacher Students are now given the opportunity in *208. You Name It:* _____, to freely compose their own melody. The only parameters given are that the melody should be in D Major and in $\frac{4}{4}$ time. Remind students that their melody will sound best to them if it is comprised of two, two bar phrases – the first one a question-sounding phrase and the second an answer-sounding phrase. Students should select a title for their composition. Feature the compositions on a concert. Students can play the world premier of their pieces!

208. YOU NAME IT: _____

Now write your own music.

THEORY

Double Stops

A **double stop** is playing two strings at once.

Teacher The technique of playing two strings at once is introduced at the top of student book page 47. Define double stops and demonstrate if possible. Students need to practice balancing and sustaining their bow on two strings as a preparation for playing double stops. The lower half of the bow is the easiest for cellos and basses, and the middle to upper half is best for violins and violas when sustaining two strings.

Playing two strings at once is a bowing skill necessary for violin, viola, and cello students to learn to tune their open strings in perfect fifths. Specific strategies for teaching students to tune their instruments are included at the end of this manual.

209. TWO AT A TIME

DOUBLE STOPS/FINGERING CHART

Teacher   In *210. Adding Fingers,* students play a pitch while sustaining an adjacent open string. These simple double stops help students learn to tune pitches to a sustained pitch.

210. ADDING FINGERS

Teacher   The following fingering charts appear on page 47 of each student book.

Violin

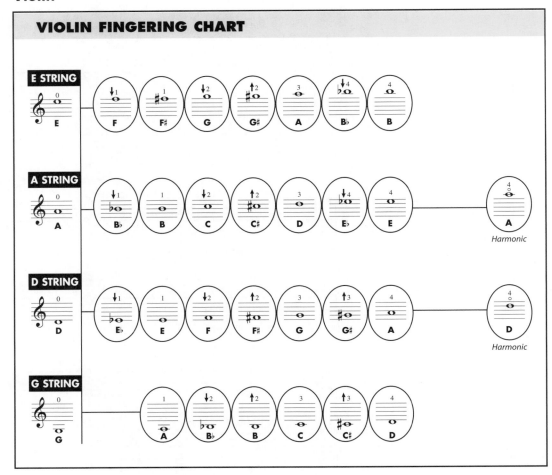

Viola

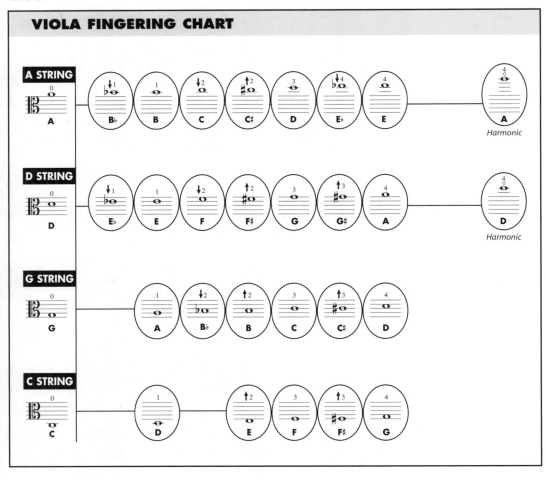

Cello

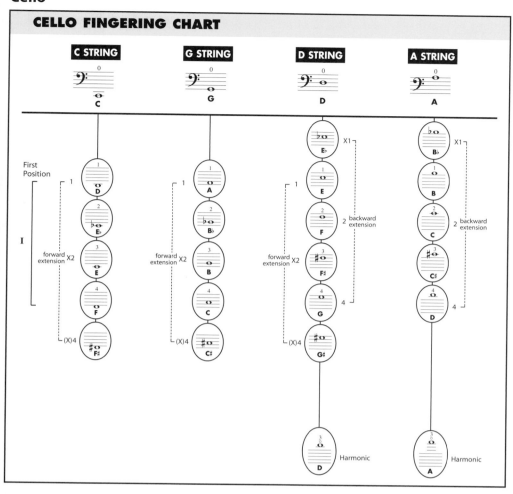

Bass

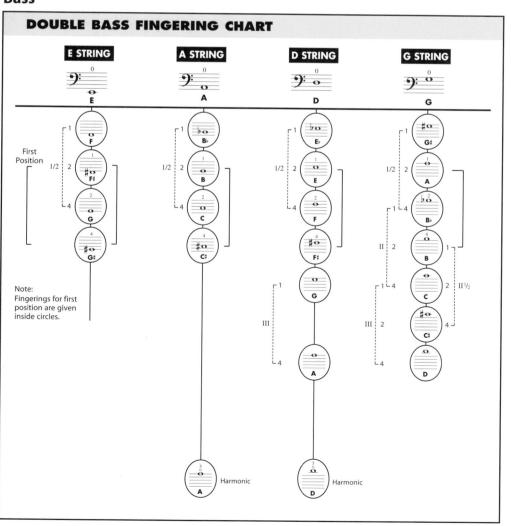

REFERENCE INDEX

WORDS TO FAMILIAR MELODIES

The following are words to some of the familiar melodies that appear throughout this method. They are provided as a resource when teaching students to play the melodies on their string instruments.

When the Saints Go Marchin' In

Oh when the saints go marching in, oh, when the saints go marching in,
Oh Lord, I want to be in that number, when the saints go marching in.

Oh, when the sun refuse to shine, oh, when the sun refuse to shine,
Oh Lord, I want to be in that number, when the sun refuse to shine.

Oh, when the stars have disappeared, oh, when the stars have disappeared,
Oh Lord, I want to be in that number, when the stars have disappeared.

Oh, when the day of judgment comes, oh, when the day of judgment comes,
Oh Lord, I want to be in that number, when the day of judgment comes.

Oh, when the saints go marching in, oh, when the saints go marching in,
Oh Lord, I want to be in that number, when the saints go marching in.

America, The Beautiful

O beautiful for spacious skies, For amber waves of grain,
For purple mountain majesties Above the fruited plain!
America! America! God shed His grace on thee,
And crown thy good with brotherhood, From sea to shining sea.

O beautiful for pilgrim feet, Whose stern, impassioned stress
A thoroughfare for freedom beat Across the wilderness!
America! America! God mend thine every flaw,
Confirm thy soul in self control, Thy liberty in law.

O beautiful for heroes proved In liberating strife,
Who more than self their country loved, and mercy more than life!
America! America! May God thy gold refine,
'Til all success be nobleness, And every gain divine.

O beautiful for patriot dream That sees beyond the years
Thine alabaster cities gleam, Undimmed by human tears!
America! America! God shed His grace on thee,
And crown thy good with brothererhood, From sea to shining sea.

Kum Ba Yah

Kum ba yah, my Lord, Kum ba yah!
Kum ba yah, my Lord, Kum ba yah!
Kum ba yah, my Lord, Kum ba yah!
Oh, Lord, Kum ba yah.

Someone's prayin', Lord, Kum ba yah!
Someone's prayin', Lord, Kum ba yah!
Someone's prayin', Lord, Kum ba yah!
Oh, Lord, Kum ba yah.

3. Someone's singin', Lord, Kum ba yah…
4. Someone's crying', Lord, Kum ba yah…
5. Someone's dancin', Lord, Kum ba yah…
6. Someone's shoutin', Lord, Kum ba yah…

Row, Row, Row Your Boat

Row, Row, Row Your Boat, Gently down the stream:
Merrily, merrily, merrily, merrily; Life is but a dream.

For He's A Jolly Good Fellow

For He's A Jolly Good Fellow, For He's A Jolly Good Fellow, For He's A Jolly Good
Fellow, Which nobody can deny, Which nobody can deny, which nobody can deny.
For He's A Jolly Good Fellow, For He's A Jolly good Fellow, For He's A Jolly Good Fellow,
Which nobody can deny.

Oh! Susannah

Well I come from Alabama with my banjo on my knee
And I'm bound for Louisiana, my own true love for to
see It did rain all night the day I left
The weather was bone dry
The sun was so hot I froze myself
Suzanne, don't you go on and cry

I said, Oh, Suzannah
Now, don't you cry for me
As I come from Alabama with this banjo on my knee

Well I had myself a dream the other night
When everything was still
I dreamed that I saw my girl Suzanne
She was coming around the hill
Now, the buckwheat cake was in her mouth
A tear was in her eye
I said, that I come from Dixie land
Suzanne, don't you break down and cry

I said, Oh, Suzannah
Now, don't you cry for me
'Cause I come from Alabama with my banjo on my
knee

Hannukah Song

Hanukah, Hanukah, hag yafeh kol kakh,
Or haviv misaviv, gil leyeled rakh.
Hanukah, Hannukah, sevivon sov, sov
Sov, sov, sov, sov, sov, sov, ma na-im va-tov.

Hatikva

As long as deep in the heart,
The soul of a Jew yearns,
And forward to the East
To Zion, an eye looks
Our hope will not be lost,
The hope of two thousand years,
To be a free nation in our land,
The land of Zion and Jerusalem.

Tom Dooley

Hang down your head, Tom Dooley
Hang down your head and cry
Hang down your head, Tom Dooley
Poor boy, you're bound to die.

Listen to the Mockingbird

Listen to the mockingbird,
Listen to the mockingbird,
The mockingbird still singing o'er her grave.
Listen to the mockingbird,
Listen to the mockingbird,
Still singing where the weeping willows wave.

GUIDELINES AND STRATEGIES FOR TUNING STRING INSTRUMENTS

Guidelines:

1. Students should purchase the best possible quality strings they can afford or that you recommend.

2. Violin students should change their E string frequently, at least twice a year.

3. All strings on the violin, viola, and cello should have fine tuners.

4. If the string is greatly out of tune, the teacher should turn the instrument peg for young students. The peg should be turned slowly and carefully. Violin and viola pegs should be positioned vertically to the peg box so that they are easier to turn. If they are not, take the string off and put more or less of the string through the peg hole.

5. Pegs must be lubricated if they are extremely difficult to turn. Apply a commercial peg lubricant to the peg.

6. Slipping pegs should be pushed into the instrument by the teacher. If the pegs still slip, check to see if the strings are touching each other in the peg box. Rearrange the pegs so that they do not touch. If there is still a problem, have a professional repair person examine the pegs.

7. It is best for the student to hold the instrument in playing position during the tuning process, even if the teacher is doing the tuning.

8. Have tuning accuracy tests and timed tuning competitions.

9. If during the group tuning process a student is unsure if a string is out of tune, the student should quit playing, listen to the other students tuning, and then join in and try to match pitch once again.

10. To prepare students for tuning their own instruments, play open string pitches for the class and have students sing the pitches. Students may also use hand signals to indicate if the pitch is sharp, flat, or in tune.

11. Demonstrate and explain to students which direction to turn the tuners to adjust the open string pitch sharper or flatter.

12. Time saving hint - Only tune the strings that will be played in class.

Sample Tuning Strategies:

1. Students strum strings with fourth finger while holding instrument in playing position, and the teacher travels throughout the class tuning the strings.

2. Teacher tunes instruments while students bow or pizzicato the rhythm of their names on open strings.

3. Sample tuning routine #1:
   - model A is sounded by student or teacher
   - all instruments tune A strings very quietly
   - all instruments tune D strings to A strings
   - all instruments sound and compare D strings
   - all instruments tune G strings to D strings
   - all instruments sound and compare G strings
   - violas and cellos tune C strings to G strings
   - violas and cellos sound and compare C strings
   - basses tune E strings to A strings
   - basses sound and compare E strings
   - violins tune E strings to A strings
   - violins sound and compare E strings

4. Sample routine #2:
   - model A is sounded by teacher or student
   - basses tune harmonic A on D string to model A
   - basses tune all strings to harmonic A
   - continue with tuning routine #1

5. Sample routine #3:
   - model A is sounded by teacher or student
   - basses tune harmonic A on D string to model A
   - basses tune all strings to harmonic A
   - violins, violas, and cellos tune A strings
   - violins stay on A while violas and cellos tune D strings to violins A
   - violas and cellos play A strings while violins tune D strings
   - violins play D strings while violas and cellos tune G strings to violins D string
   - violas and cellos play D strings while violins tune G strings
   - violins play G strings while violas and cellos tune C strings to violins G string
   - violas and cellos play A strings while violins tune E strings

Teacher The following are the tempos that have been introduced in *Essential Elements 2000 for Strings,* books 1 and 2. Feel free to make photocopies of this chart for use by your students. It may be helpful for them to see how the tempos relate to each other. Enough space has been allowed for the student to add new tempos to the chart as they are learned.

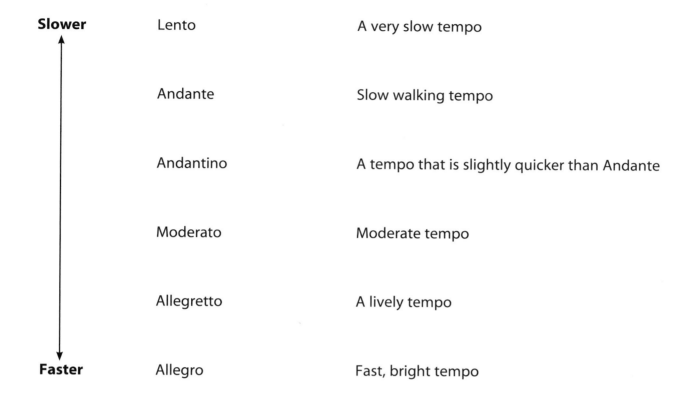

Slower

Lento — A very slow tempo

Andante — Slow walking tempo

Andantino — A tempo that is slightly quicker than Andante

Moderato — Moderate tempo

Allegretto — A lively tempo

Faster — Allegro — Fast, bright tempo

GUIDELINES FOR SELECTING THE CORRECT SIZED STRING INSTRUMENT FOR YOUR STUDENTS

Instrument	Size	Left Hand Span (Between pinky and index fingers)	Left Arm Length (From shoulder sleeve to end of middle finger)	Height
Violin	Full	5–6 inches	over 24 inches	
	3/4	4 1/2–5 inches	21–24 inches	
	1/2	4–4 1/2 inches	18–21 inches	
	1/4	3 1/2–4 inches	under 18 inches	
*Viola	16 inch	6 inches or more	28 inches or more	
	15 1/2 inch	6 inches	26–27 inches	
	15 inch	5–6 inches	25 inches	
	14 inch	5–6 inches	24 inches	
	13 1/4 inch	4 1/2–5 inches	21–24 inches	
Cello	Full	6 inches	24 inches	60 inches
	3/4	5 inches	22 inches	56 inches
	1/2	4 inches	20 inches	52 inches
	1/4	3 inches	18 inches	48 inches
Bass	3/4	6 1/2 inches	24 inches	over 60 inches
	1/2	5 3/4 inches	22 inches	56 inches
	1/4	5 inches	20 inches	52 inches

* A 3/4 violin and a junior viola are the same length. A full size violin is the same length as an intermediate viola.

Teacher The following are standards established by the American String Teachers Association with the National School Orchestra Association for successful string/orchestra teaching in the schools. Use the standards as goals and guidelines in evaluating and developing your teaching skills.

AMERICAN STRING TEACHERS ASSOCIATION with NATIONAL SCHOOL ORCHESTRA ASSOCIATION

STANDARDS FOR SUCCESSFUL SCHOOL STRING/ORCHESTRA TEACHING

I. As a Musician

1. demonstrates a high level of musicianship in performance

2. performs at an intermediate to advanced level on at least one string instrument

3. demonstrates at least basic to intermediate performance concepts on one string instrument and understands advanced and artistic concepts on other string instruments

4. demonstrates ability to play by ear and improvise

5. demonstrates a basic knowledge of performing and teaching the woodwind, brass, and percussion instruments at least at a basic level, with an understanding of intermediate to advanced concepts

6. demonstrates orchestral conducting skills

7. demonstrates keyboard skills of at least a basic to intermediate level and accompanies melodies using at least I-IV-V chords

8. demonstrates aural discrimination skills

9. demonstrates the understanding of prevention of performance injuries

10. demonstrates the knowledge of a wide range of music repertoire for teaching diverse styles, genres, cultures and historical periods

II. As an Educator

1. understands and applies pedagogy for violin, viola, cello and bass

2. demonstrates effective rehearsal techniques for string and full orchestra

3. demonstrates the knowledge of a variety of string and orchestral instruction materials at all levels

4. demonstrates the knowledge of repertoire for student performance, including solo literature, orchestra music, and chamber music

5. demonstrates skill in arranging music for school orchestras

6. demonstrates strategies for integrating music with other disciplines

7. understands different student learning styles, levels of maturation, special needs, and adapts instruction accordingly

8. demonstrates knowledge of comprehensive, sequential K-12 music curricula, including string and orchestra, with appropriate goals and expectations for all levels of proficiencies

9. demonstrates understanding of the principles of a variety of homogeneous and heterogeneous pedagogical approaches for teaching string classes (Suzuki, Rolland, Bornoff, e.g.)

10. exhibits effective classroom management skills and strategies

11. demonstrates understanding of how to teach students of diverse ages, socio-economic, ethnic, and geographic backgrounds

12. demonstrates effective methods of assessing and evaluating student achievement

13. knows about instrument rental and purchasing

14. knows current technology for instruction, research, and musical applications

15. knows of current music and general education policies, including current scheduling practices for successful string and orchestra programs

16. demonstrates ability to gather pertinent orchestra program data

17. understands the importance of maintaining a balance between personal and career interests

18. demonstrates ability to develop budgets for equipment and supplies

19. demonstrates understanding of effective advocacy strategies for comprehensive music programs which include string/orchestra programs

20. demonstrates clear communication in written and oral form

21. demonstrates understanding of the K-12 National Music Education Standards and other state and local standards for music

III. As a Professional

A. Musician

1. continues to perform

2. demonstrates concepts and understandings necessary for student achievement of Grade 12 National Music Education Standards

3. exhibits effective, on-going professional self-assessment

4. continues to pursue opportunities for learning as a musician

B. Professional Affiliations and Related Activities

1. maintains active involvement in professional associations, such as MENC, ASTA/NSOA, SSA, CMA

2. continues to interact with other music educators, observes other programs

3. demonstrates professional ethics, appearance, behavior, and relationships within the profession, the school, and greater community

4. participates in ongoing professional development to improve teaching effectiveness

5. serves in leadership roles with state and local MEA's, ASTA/NSOA chapters

C. School and Community Relations

1. develops a healthy rapport with school administrators for nurturing a successful string and orchestra program

2. understands the value of positive interaction with other members of the music and arts community

3. establishes and maintains positive relations with school administrators, staff, and fellow teachers through communication and dialogue

4. articulates the positive aspects of the string/orchestra component of a school music program through writing and speaking

5. communicates effectively with parent support/booster groups, including clear and grammatically correct communication

6. advocates effectively for a strong school orchestra program

Teacher The following bibliography lists the resources considered essential by the Professional String Teaching and Playing Association (ASTA with NSOA).

AMERICAN STRING TEACHERS ASSOCIATION with the NATIONAL SCHOOL ORCHESTRA ASSOCIATION

ESSENTIAL RESOURCE LIST FOR STRING TEACHERS

Stringed Instruments: Instruction and Study

The Complete String Guide: Standards, Programs, Purchase, and Maintenance. (1988). Reston, VA: Music Educators National Conference.

Dillon, J. & Kriechbaum, C. (1978). How to Design and Teach a Successful School String and Orchestra Program. San Diego, CA: Kjos West.

Dillon-Krass, J. & Straub, D. A. (Compilers). (1991). TIPS: Establishing a String and Orchestra Program. Reston, VA: Music Educators National Conference.

Green, E. A. (1966). Teaching Stringed Instruments in Classes. Englewood Cliff, NJ: Prentice-Hall, Inc. (available through ASTA).

Goodrich, K. & Wagner. M. (2003). Getting It Right From the Start: A Guide to Beginning and and Enriching A Successful String Orchestra Program. 2nd ed. Washington, DC: American String Teachers Association.

Guidelines for Performances of School Music Groups: Expectations and Limitations. (1986) Reston, VA: Music Educators National Conference.

A Guide to Teaching Strings. Dubuque, IA: Wm. C. Brown and Co.

Mullins, S. (1998). Teaching Music: The Human Experience. Dallas, TX: Tarrant Dallas Printing.

Teaching String Instruments: A Course of Study. (1991). MENC Task Force on String Education. Reston, VA: Music Educators National Conference.

Highlights from the ASTA School Teacher's Forum. (1984-1994). Bloomington, IN: Tichenor Publishing.

String Syllabus. (revised 1997). ASTA. Bloomington, IN: Tichenor Publishing.

Straub, D. A., Bergonzi, L., & Witt, A. C. (Eds.). (1996). Strategies for Teaching Strings and Orchestra. Reston, VA: Music Educators National Conference.

Young, P. (1978). Playing the String Game - Strategies for Teaching Cello and Strings. Ann Arbor, MI: Shar Music.

Young, P. (1985). The String Play - The Drama of Playing and Teaching Strings. Austin, TX: University of Texas Press.

Strings, Winds, Brass, and Percussion
Managing the Instrumental Music Program

Colwell, R. J. and Goolsby, T. (1992). The Teaching of Instrumental Music. Englewood Cliffs, NJ: Prentice Hall.

Goodrich, K. & Wagner. M. (2003). Getting It Right From the Start: A Guide to Beginning and and Enriching A Successful String Orchestra Program. 2nd ed. Washington, DC: American String Teachers Association.

Kohut, D. L. (1973). Instrumental Music Pedagogy: Teaching Techniques for School Band and Orchestra Directors. Englewood Cliffs, NJ: Prentice-Hall.

Strategies for Success in the Band and Orchestra. (1994). Reston, VA: Music Educators National Conference.

Walker, D. E. (1988). Teaching Music: Managing the Successful Music Program. New York, NY: Schirmer Books.

String Class Materials

Method Books

Allen, M., Gillespie, R., & Hayes, P.T. Essential Elements for Strings, (1995) Books I, II, and the Teacher Resource Kit, and Essential Techniques for Strings. Milwaukee, WI: Hal Leonard Corporation.

Anderson, G. & Frost, R. (1986). All for Strings. Kjos. Supplementary materials available.

Applebaum, S. Applebaum String Method. Books I, II, III. New York, NY: Belwin-Mills. Books I - III. Supplementary Applebaum materials include the following: Etudes for Technique and Musicianship, Chamber Music for Two String Instruments, Chamber Music for String Orchestra, and Solos with Piano Accompaniment.

Dabczynski, A., Meyer, R., & Philiips, B. (2002). String Explorer. Books I and II. Highland/Etling Pub. (a division of Alfred Music Publishing).

Dillon, J., Kjelland, J. & O'Reilly, J. Strictly Strings. Books I, II and III. Highland/Etling Pub. (a division of Alfred Music Publishing). Supplementary materials available.

Etling, F. String Method, Books I and II; Intermediate String Techniques; Solo Time for Strings, Books I, II, III, IV, and V; Workbook for Strings, Books I and II.

Froseth & Johnson (1981). Introducing the Strings, G.I.A. Publications.

Frost, R., & Fischbach, G. (2002). Artistry in Strings. Books I and II. San Diego, CA: Neil A. Kjos Music Company.

Gazda, D. & Stoutamire, A. (1997). Spotlight on Strings. San Diego, CA: Neil A. Kjos Music Company.

Isaac, M. (1962) String Class Method. Chicago, IL: M. M. Cole. Books I and II.

Matesky, R. & Womack, A. (1971). Learn to Play a Stringed Instrument. New York, NY: Alfred Music Co. Books I, II, and III.

Matesky, R. Learn to Play in the Orchestra. (1971). New York, NY: Alfred Music Co. Volumes I and II

Muller, F. & Rusch, H. Muller-Rusch String Method. (1961). Books I - V plus supplementary materials: ensembles, solos, etc. San Diego, CA: Neil A. Kjos Music Co.

Music Lists for Orchestra/String Orchestra

Non-Graded:

Farrish, M. K. (1965). String Music in Print. New York, NY: R. R. Bowker.

Farrish, M. K. (1968). Supplement to String Music in Print. New York, NY: R. R. Bowker.

Farrish, M. K. (1979). Orchestral Music in Print: Educational Section. Philadelphia, PA: Musicdata.

Littrell, D. & Racin, L. (2001) Teaching Music Through Performance in Orchestra. Chicago, IL: GIA Publications, Inc.

Graded Lists:

Matesky, R. & Smith, J. (1979). ASTA - NSOA Compendium of Orchestra & String Orchestra Literature: 1959-1977. Reston, VA: American String Teachers Association.

Mayer, F. R. (Ed.). (1993). The String Orchestra Super List. Reston, VA: Music Educators National Conference.

National School Orchestra Association - Sure-Fire Materials for the First-Year Orchestra Director.

NOTE: *Many state organizations have graded music lists available.*

National Standards for Arts Education

Allen, M. L. (1995). "The national standards for arts education: Implications for school string programs." American String Teacher, 45 (2), 30.

Bergonzi, L. (1996). "School teachers: The national standards in music: Access to string study for all children." American String Teacher, 46 (2), 69.

Dabczynski, A. H. (1995). "National standards for arts education: A golden opportunity for string teachers." American String Teacher, 45 (1), 73.

Daugherty, E. (1995). "Editorial: Implementing national standards in music: Context challenges and opportunities." The Quarterly of the Center for Research in Music Education, 6 (2), 3.

Kjelland, J. (1995). "String teacher preparation and the national music standards." American String Teacher, 45 (4), 34.

Mark, M. L. (1995). "Music education and the national standards: A historical review." The Quarterly of the Center for Research in Music Education, 6 (2), 34.

National Standards for Arts Education: What Every Young American Should Know and Be Able to Do in the Arts. Reston, VA: Music Educators National Conference.

Opportunity-to-Learn Standards for Music Instruction: Grades Pre K-12. (1994) Reston, VA: Music Educators National Conference.

Performance Standards for Music: Strategies and Benchmarks for Assessing Progress Toward the National Standards, Grades Pre K-12. (1996) Reston, VA: Music Educators National Conference.

The School Music Program: A New Vision. (1994). Reston, VA: Music Educators National Conference.

Shuler, S. C. (1995). "The impact of national standards on the preparation, in-service professional development, and assessment of music teachers." Arts Education Policy Review, 96 (3), 2.

Straub, D. A. (1995). "The national standards for art education: context and issues." American String Teacher, 45 (3), 24. Straub, D. A., Bergonzi, L., & Witt, A. C. (Eds.) (1996) Strategies for Teaching Strings and Orchestra. Reston, VA: Music Educators National Conference.

Advocacy

Action Kit for Music Education. (1991). Reston, VA: Music Educators National Conference. (brochures, books, videos)

Does Your School District Have an Orchestra Program? (1993). Reston, VA: Music Educators National Conference. (brochure)

Day, S. H. (1996). "Teaching orchestra on a year-round schedule." Teaching Music, 4, 33-35.

Kendall, S. (1997). "Securing our string programs." American String Teacher, 47 (2), 47.

Tellejohn, P. (1989). "Ensure your string program's success." American String Teacher, 76 (2), 30-32.

Scheduling Time for Music. (1995). Reston, VA: Music Educators National Conference.

Pedagogical Videos

From University of Wisconsin, Division of University Outreach, Department of Continuing Education.

Rabin, M. , et al. (1986). Rabin on Strings.

Rabin, M. & Smith, P. (1984). Guide to Orchestral Bowings Through Music Styles.

Paul Rolland

Rolland, P. Basic Principles of Violin Playing. (MENC Publication, 1959: ASTA, 1983).

Rolland, P. and Mutschler, M. (1974). The Teaching of Action in String Playing: Developmental and Remedial Techniques. Urbana, IL: Illinois String Research Associates.

Film

University of Illinois Film Series on Teaching of Action in String Playing. Urbana, IL: Illinois String Research Associates. Fourteen 16mm color films or videotapes; artists, teachers, and students demonstrate principles of Teaching of Action in String Playing.

String Repair

Bearden, L. & Bearden, D. (1972). Emergency String Repair Manual, 2nd Edition. AL: The University of Alabama Press.

Weisshaar, O. H. (1966). Preventative Maintenance of Stringed Instruments. Rockville Center, MD: Belwin, Inc.

Zurfluh, J. D. (Ed.). (1978). String Instrument Repair and Maintenance Manual. American String Teachers Association.

Bowing

Green, E. A. (1957). Orchestra Bowings and Routines - 2nd edition. (18th Printing). Reston, VA: American String Teachers Association.

Berman, J., Jackson and Sarah K. ASTA Dictionary of Bowing/Pizzicato Terms and Techniques (4th Edition). 1998. Bloomington, IN: Tichenor Publishing.

Video-Tape

Rabin, M. & Smith, P. (1991). Guide to Orchestral Bowings through Music Styles. Madison, WI: University of Wisconsin-Extension.

Pedagogical Concerns

From *American String Teacher*

Allen, M. L. (1994). "Introducing and integrating basic skills in the beginning string class." American String Teacher, 44 (3), 69-72.

Fischbach, G. "Getting from here to there with a smile: A sequential outline of the skills of shifting for business and pleasure." American String Teacher.
Three part article:
 I. Basic Principles, Summer 1980, 30 (3), 11-12.
 II. Sequential Course of Study. Autumn, 1980, 30 (4), 28-30.
 III. Shifting for Pleasure, Winter 1981, 31(1), 12-13.

Gillespie, R. (1997). "String teacher training: Using history to guide the future." American String Teacher, 47 (1), 62-66.

Moskovitz, M. D. (1997). "Making the connection: Shifting through hand positions." American String Teacher, 47 (3), 55-58.

From *The Instrumentalist*

Burgess, N. (1977). "Fiddling for technical development." The Instrumentalist. 32 (5), 81-83.

Gillespie, R. (1989). "Teaching spiccato to string classes: Effective strategies for teaching your group the spiccato bounce." The Instrumentalist, 44 (4), 52, 56, 59-60.

Gillespie, R. (1992). "Building a Bass Section." The Instrumentalist, 47 (5), 66-69.

Grieve, T. (1989). "Fresh approaches to scale practice." The Instrumentalist, 43 (7), 44-46.

Rejto, G. (1978). "Strings: Producing a beautiful string tone." The Instrumentalist, 33 (2), 76.

Journals

American String Teacher
American String Teachers Association (ASTA)
with the National School Orchestra Association (NSOA)
4153 Chain Bridge Road
Fairfax, VA 22030

The Instrumentalist
200 Northfield Road
Northfield, IL 60093

Music Educators Journal
Music Educators National Conference
1806 Robert Fulton Drive
Reston, VA 22091-4348

Teaching Music
Music Educators National Conference
1806 Robert Fulton Drive
Reston, VA 22091-4348

Professional Organizations

American String Teachers Association (ASTA) with the National School Orchestra
Association (NSOA)
4153 Chain Bridge Road
Fairfax, VA 22030
www.astaweb.com

Music Educators National Conference
1806 Robert Fulton Drive
Reston, VA 22091-4348
www.menc.org

Suzuki Association of the Americas
P.O. Box 17310
Boulder, CO 80308

Teacher   The following are video training programs for developing skills to diagnose and solve string students playing skills.

Video String Teacher Teaching Programs

Contact Robert Gillespie for these materials:
Ohio State University School of Music
110 Weigel Hall
1866 College Road
Columbus, OH 43210-1170
gillespie.5@osu.edu

Gillespie, Robert. The Violin Bowing Diagnostic Skills Program. Two videotapes and manual designed to train and evaluate teachers' abilities to recognize and solve common bowing problems of beginning violin students. Available for rent or purchase through the ASTA Media Resource Center.

Gillespie, Robert. The Violin Instrument Position and Left Hand Skills Training Program. A videotape and manual designed to train teachers to recognize common instrument position and left hand skills problems of beginning and intermediate violin students. Available for rent or purchase through the ASTA Media Resource Center.

Gillespie, Robert, William Conable, and Brent Wilson. The Cello Diagnostic Skills Training Program. A videotape and manual designed to train teachers to recognize common instrument position and left hand fingering problems of beginning and intermediate cello students. Available for rent or purchase through the ASTA Media Resource Center.

Authors

MICHAEL ALLEN
Professor of Music Education, Florida State University, Tallahassee, FL

ROBERT GILLESPIE
Professor of Music, The Ohio State University, Columbus, OH

PAMELA TELLEJOHN HAYES
Orchestra Coordinator (retired), Richland School District Two, Columbia, SC

JOHN HIGGINS
Managing Producer and Editor, Composer and Arranger, Hal Leonard Corp., Milwaukee, WI

Credits

Managing Editor and Producer	Paul Lavender
Production Editor	Stuart Malavsky
Orchestra Arrangements	John Higgins
Design and Art Direction	Richard Slater Tim Begonia
Music Engraving and Typesetting	Thomas Schaller
Play-Along Trax Arrangements and Production	Paul Lavender
Additional Arrangements	John Moss Larry Moore
Essential Elements Rhythm Section	Steve Millikan - Keyboards Steve Potts - Keyboards Steve Dokken - Bass Sandy Williams - Guitars Steve Hanna - Percussion Larry Sauer - Drums
Recording and Mixing Engineers **Aire Born Studios, Indianapolis, IN**	Mark Aspinall John Bolt David Price Ben Vawter Mike Wilson
Additional Recording Production	Jared Rodin Mark Aspinall
Project Supervision **Aire Born Studios, Indianapolis, IN**	Nanci Milam Mike Wilson Nina Hunt
Announcer	Scott Hoke

The authors wish to give special thanks to Herman Knoll Senior, Vice President of Hal Leonard,
for his dedication, leadership, and expertise in the creation of the Essential Elements educational program.

Notes

Notes